THE SOUTH OF
FRANCE
COOKBOOK

THE SOUTH OF
FRANCE
COOKBOOK

Recipes and stories from St. Tropez

NINA PARKER

weldon**owen**

INTRODUCTION

IT ALL STARTED when my parents met on the beaches of St. Tropez during the summer holidays when they were young. Since then, my family has continued to come to this beautiful little fishing town every year, and I haven't spent a single summer away from it since I was born. This book is my personal food-themed journey around the historic seaside town and surrounding area. In my 1970s Citroën van, on our neighbor's boat and at times on my trusty bicycle, I love to explore Provençal cuisine and create recipes inspired by the locals, places and stories of my summers here. I am passionate about the Riviera style of cooking: strong, fresh flavors and colorful food that is, above all, utterly delicious.

The St. Tropez of today retains echoes of its long history and traditions. It's full of artists, fishermen, vineyards, secret cycle tracks and bric-a-brac markets, as well as amazing restaurants, purveyors and neighborhoods creating wonderful food far off the beaten track. I want to show you the classic, often-forgotten side of town, far away from the mega-yachts and spray of Champagne; from Le Mazagran's unique homemade ratatouille, Elvis's smoky, wafer-thin Provençal pizza, Jacques Feline's Bouillabaisse, and the chefs at Sénéquier bakery as they roll out the croissants at 4am to happy times spent eating at Del-Rey's ice-cream parlor. This is not the new St. Tropez, it's the real St. Tropez; much of it has remained intact since its heyday in the 1950s, holding on to that old-world charm and glamour all the while.

These chapters feature places that I have visited my whole life. Here, you'll find my take on the classic recipes of the south of France, from easy-to-cook dishes for gourmet breakfasts to picnic lunches, lavish teatimes and dinner parties to impress.

Through its mouthwatering food, fascinating heritage and stunning scenery, I want you to discover the St. Tropez I fall in love with summer after summer.

BREAKFAST
PETIT DÉJEUNER

BREAKFAST IS AN important event in the south of France. It's often an extremely indulgent occasion when everyone comes together for a buttery, pastry-layered, jam-fueled extravaganza. My favorite St. Tropez breakfast stop is the Sénéquier bakery, where I once spent a long, hot summer in the kitchen making croissants. These days I'm more likely to enjoy a bit of people-watching on its terrace over a delightful *petit déjeuner complet*. Another of my favorites is the charming Café de l'Ormeau at the top of Ramatuelle village; time has not touched this place since the 1950s.

I'm excited about sharing my own signature croissant recipe. Croissants are utterly worth their weight in gold, completely worth the effort, and when these emerge from the oven, you'll be instantly transported to the south of France. They should be slathered with only the most heavenly spreads and jams, many of which have been inspired by trips to out-of-the-way delicatessens in Grimaud village and La Maison des Confitures, the astounding 400-flavor collection of jam that Peter Mayle wrote about in *A Year in Provence*.

If you're not yet convinced about the importance of delicious things for breakfast, have I mentioned my Sticky Buns? These could perhaps even rival some of the all-time greats, such as brioche and *pain au chocolat*. Oh-so-sticky honey and pecan buns with a subtle hint of fennel, these bad boys are perfect with coffee. Bread is not the only direction you can go in though: I can't urge you strongly enough to try the Chestnut Festival Crêpes from La Garde-Freinet. They're delicate in flavor, give off an incredibly nutty aroma, and are out of this world served with my Sea-Salted Caramel from Grimaud. This is breakfast at its absolute best!

BRIOCHE DE RAMATUELLE | RAMATUELLE BRIOCHE

MAKES 1 LARGE OR 2 SMALL LOAVES

5 tsp whole milk
2 tsp fresh yeast,
or 1¼ tsp instant yeast
1¼ cups (6½ oz/200 g) bread flour
2 free-range large eggs, plus
2 yolks, lightly beaten
2 tbsp unrefined superfine sugar
½ cup (4 oz/125 g) soft
unsalted butter
sea salt

When I think of Ramatuelle, I think of breakfast. A bike ride to Ramatuelle with our father has been a tradition of my sister's and mine since we were little. A winner's breakfast of fresh brioche, butter and apricot jam at the Café de l'Ormeau at the top of the hill is the ultimate incentive! The place hasn't changed in 50 years, and it has inspired me to make my own brioche. It can be made by hand, but it's much easier to use an electric stand mixer. Once you've mastered the loaf, you can buy brioche molds and make the iconic brioche shape.

Heat the milk until lukewarm and add the yeast and 1 heaped teaspoon of the flour. Set aside for 30 minutes, covered with plastic wrap.

In the bowl of a stand mixer, beat three-quarters of the eggs, the sugar and a pinch of salt together. Add the yeast mixture, and after a minute, gradually spoon in the rest of the flour. Mix until everything is just combined, then cover with a tea towel and leave to rest for 30 minutes. Now, set the mixer to a slow speed and begin spooning in the soft butter, letting each addition combine with the dough before adding the next. Once everything is incorporated, increase the speed and mix until the dough looks elastic and shiny. Scrape into a clean, dry bowl, cover with plastic wrap and leave to rise in the fridge overnight.

The next day, line a slightly larger-than-standard loaf pan, or two standard 8 x 4 x 2½-inch (17 x 11 x 8-cm) pans, with parchment paper. Take the dough out of the fridge and put it in the pan(s). Cover lightly with plastic wrap and leave to proof for 2-3 hours in a warm, dry place. Preheat the oven to 400°F (200°C). Once the dough has doubled in size, brush it with the remaining beaten egg and bake it for 20-25 minutes, or until the top is gorgeous and golden. Remove and allow to cool completely on a wire rack. Serve warm with Apricot and Almond Jam (page 18) or Sea-Salted Caramel from Grimaud (page 23).

CROISSANTS DE SÉNÉQUIER | SÉNÉQUIER CROISSANTS

MAKES ABOUT 20

3¼ cups (16 oz/500 g) bread flour, sifted, plus extra for dusting
⅓ cup (2½ oz/70 g) unrefined superfine sugar
1 tsp salt
scant 2 tbsp fresh yeast or 1 package (2½ tsp) instant yeast, dissolved in 2 tbsp lukewarm water
3½ tbsp (1¾ oz/50 g) soft unsalted butter, plus ¾ cup plus 2 tbsp (6½ oz/200 g) cold unsalted butter
6½ tbsp (3½ fl oz/100 ml) whole milk, plus 2 tbsp for the egg wash
½ cup plus 1 tbsp (4½ fl oz/140 ml) tepid water
1 free-range large egg

I managed to persuade one of the chefs to let me do a stage (work experience placement) at the Sénéquier pâtisserie, one of the most famous bakeries in the region. I love the fact that the kitchen doesn't look as though it has changed much since it first opened in 1887. The proofing process takes three days to create the perfect, buttery layers of pastry, and in peak season the bakery sells 150 to 170 croissants per day. After work I would walk home with a warm paper bag full of them. They were seriously the best I've ever tasted. The recipe isn't difficult, but you'll need an electric stand mixer, and good-quality butter makes all the difference.

Pour the flour, sugar, salt, yeast, soft butter, the 6½ tbsp (3½ fl oz/100 ml) milk and the water into a stand mixer bowl and beat at medium speed, gradually increasing it, for about 5 minutes. It should come together into a ball. Lightly flour a surface and knead for 5 minutes. The key throughout the process is not to add too much flour. Roll it into a ball and place on a sheet pan lined with parchment paper. Cut a cross into the ball with a sharp knife, cover with plastic wrap and leave in a warm, dry place to rise for 30 minutes.

Turn the dough onto a lightly floured surface and roll out into a rectangle, ⅔–¾ inch (1.5–2cm) thick. Return to the sheet pan, cover with plastic wrap, and place in the fridge for 2 hours.

Roll out the cold butter into a square the same width as the dough. It helps to do this between two sheets of parchment paper. The butter will need to fit perfectly inside the rectangle, so trim off any uneven edges and press them back into the center. Place the dough on the floured surface and put the square of cold butter in the center. Fold both ends of the dough over the butter so they meet each other in the center without overlapping or leaving a gap.

Bash it gently with the rolling pin, squashing the layers together, then roll it out again, keeping the rectangle shape. Now fold the two ends in again and bash it with the rolling pin to squash it together. Take one edge and fold it two-thirds

inward, then fold the other end to meet it. Lastly, fold it in half and bash with the rolling pin to push it together. Keep it covered in the fridge overnight. This process of folding creates the buttery layers.

The next day, roll out the dough, keeping the rectangle shape. Fold the two ends inward to meet in a single layer and bash it with the rolling pin as before. Leave to proof for 30 minutes in the fridge. On a lightly floured surface, roll out the dough to ½ inch (1–1.5 cm) thick, keeping the rectangle shape. Using a butter knife, cut the dough straight along the middle, making two long strips of dough. Set one strip aside and cut the other into 10 or 11 long triangles. In the center of the base of each triangle, cut a ½-inch (1-cm) slit, fold the edges of the slit outward and continue rolling. This folds into the familiar croissant shape. Finish shaping all the triangles and do the same with the second strip of dough. Place the croissants on two baking sheets lined with parchment paper, cover with plastic wrap and put in a warm, dry place to proof for 1½–2 hours. They should double in size.

Preheat the oven to 350°F (180°C). Beat the egg with the 2 tablespoons milk to make a glaze. Using a pastry brush, lightly brush the glaze over the croissants and bake for 10–15 minutes, or until golden brown. Serve immediately with butter and jam. They can be reheated the next day to freshen them up.

LE STICKY BUN | STICKY BUNS

MAKES ABOUT 24

FOR THE BUNS
3¼ cups (16 oz/500 g) bread flour, plus extra for dusting
finely grated zest of 1 unwaxed lemon
1¾ cups (14 fl oz/400 ml) whole or low-fat milk
3½ tbsp (1¾ oz/50 g) soft unsalted butter
⅔ cup (5 oz/160 g) unrefined superfine sugar
2 free-range large eggs
scant 3 tbsp fresh yeast, or 1 package (2½ tsp) instant yeast
2½ tsp ground cinnamon
½ tsp salt

FOR THE BUTTER FILLING
6½ tbsp (3½ oz/100 g) unsalted butter, softened
2 tbsp honey
2 tbsp unrefined superfine sugar
2 tsp ground cinnamon
2 tsp poppy seeds
2 tsp fennel seeds

FOR THE GLAZE
1 cup (3½ oz/100 g) pecan halves
7 tbsp (3½ oz/100 g) unsalted butter
4½ tbsp (3½ oz/100 g) honey

These are really worth the time and effort because you will be rewarded with the ultimate extravagant, gooey buns to devour with coffee. They do not disappoint.

To make the buns, put ¼ cup (1½ oz/50 g) of the flour and the lemon zest in a saucepan and slowly add the milk, whisking to form a paste. Once all the flour is dissolved and there are no lumps, stir in any remaining milk, put the pan over high heat and whisk constantly. (If using fresh yeast, reserve 2 tablespoons of the milk, heat it until lukewarm, dissolve the yeast in it and set it aside to bubble; add it later along with the sugar and eggs.) The mixture will thicken after a couple of minutes, and eventually it will begin to boil. At this point, remove it and scrape everything into a mixing bowl, stir in the butter and leave to cool for 10 minutes.

Once the mixture feels lukewarm to the touch, stir in the sugar, 1 of the eggs and the yeast, followed by the cinnamon and salt. Gradually incorporate the remaining flour, then bring it all together with your hands to form a dough. When everything is combined, cover with plastic wrap and leave for 10 minutes. Lightly flour a work surface and knead the dough for about 10 minutes, then cover and leave for another 10 minutes. Repeat twice more. This technique is important because it will give the dough a beautiful, fluffy center. After the final knead, place the dough in a clean bowl, cover and leave in a warm, dry place for 1 hour or so, until doubled in size.

To make the filling, whip together the butter, honey and sugar, then add the cinnamon and seeds. Line a baking pan with parchment paper. Once the dough has risen, knock it back by punching it with your fist to release the air. Turn it out onto a lightly floured surface and roll into a long rectangle about ⅜ inch (1 cm) thick. With the back of a spoon, spread the butter paste over the dough, then roll it up tightly from one long side of the rectangle to make a long sausage shape. Use a butter knife to cut it into ¾-inch (2-cm) pieces and place the rolls, cut side up and just touching one another, on the

pan. Cover loosely with plastic wrap or a clean tea towel and leave to proof for 45 minutes to 1 hour, until doubled in size.

Meanwhile, preheat the oven to 350°F (180°C). Toast the pecans in the oven for about 10 minutes, then remove and set aside. Increase the oven temperature to 400°F (200°C). Beat the remaining egg in a small bowl. Uncover the risen buns and brush them with the egg, then bake for 15 minutes, or until golden brown all over.

While the buns cook, put the butter and honey in a saucepan over a high heat and cook until it bubbles. Remove from the heat, roughly chop the toasted pecans and stir them in. Once the buns come out of the oven, drizzle this heavenly glaze over them. Eat while warm! Covered, they keep well until the next day and can be reheated.

PAIN À LA NOIX DE COCO ET AU MIEL SAUVAGE | COCONUT AND WILD HONEY BREAD

MAKES 2 LOAVES

5½ tbsp (2¾ oz/80 g) unsalted butter, melted, plus extra for greasing
¾ cup plus 1 tbsp (3½ oz/100 g) ground almonds
1¾ cups (6½ oz/200 g) coconut flour
1¼ cups (3½ oz/100 g) unsweetened coconut flakes, or scant 1 cup (3½ oz/100 g) unsweetened shredded dried coconut
2 tsp baking powder
1 tsp ground cinnamon
few gratings nutmeg
½ cup (3½ oz/100 g) unrefined superfine sugar
1 vanilla bean
6½ tbsp (3½ fl oz/100 ml) wild honey
1 cup plus 2 tbsp (9 fl oz/280 ml) whole milk
4 free-range large eggs
sea salt

I'll admit it: coconut is one of my vices. I never seem to tire of its subtle but iconic flavor, whether savory or sweet. In France it's normally the latter, and this wheat-free loaf is pretty special. Served by itself, with butter, or toasted with honey or Apricot and Almond Jam (page 18), it's a welcome change from all the tempting and decadent pastries out there.

Preheat the oven to 325°F (170°C). Butter and line two 8 x 4 x 2½-inch (17 x 11 x 8-cm) loaf pans with parchment paper. I find it easier to cut the paper into two 6 x 14-inch (15 x 35-cm) pieces so that you can pry the loaf out by later pulling on the overhanging flaps.

Mix together all the dry ingredients and a pinch of salt in a large mixing bowl. Split the vanilla bean in half lengthwise and scrape out the seeds with the back of a knife into the bowl. Mix the honey and milk together and stir half into the bowl. Break in 2 of the eggs and combine. Now slowly stir in the remaining milk and honey, and add the last 2 eggs and the melted butter. Mix until the batter is just combined. Do not be tempted to overbeat. Scrape it into the prepared pans and bake in the oven for about 1½ hours, or until a skewer comes out fairly clean. I usually cover the pans with aluminum foil after 1 hour to prevent the top from burning. The loaves will seem a little soft, but leave them to cool for 10 minutes before turning out onto a wire rack to cool completely. They will keep for 4 days in an airtight container.

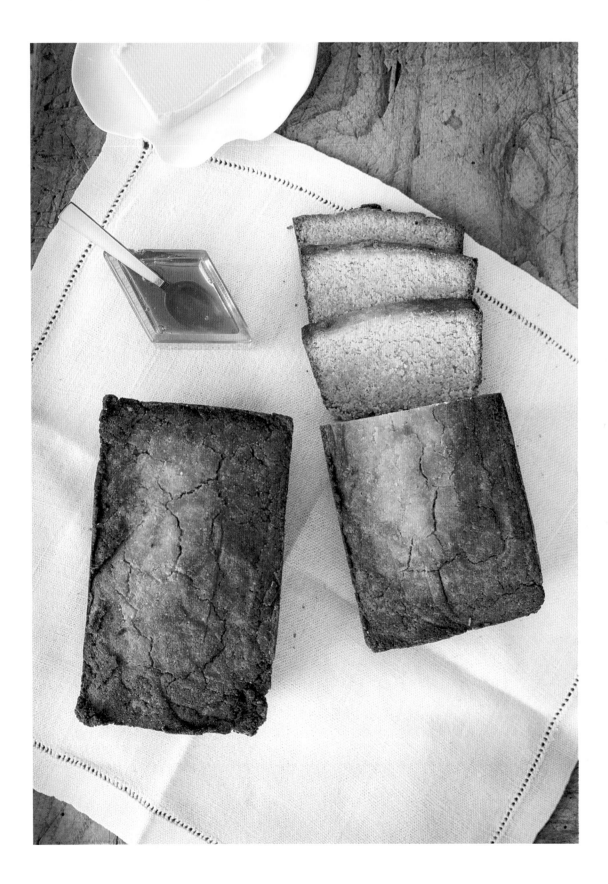

CONFITURE D'ABRICOTS AUX AMANDES | APRICOT AND ALMOND JAM

**MAKES 4 JARS
(8 FL OZ/250 ML EACH)**

¼ lb (625 g) apricots (about 12-13)
about 2 cups (13 oz/400 g)
superfine sugar (depending on
the sweetness of the fruit)
scant 1 cup (3½ oz/100 g) sliced
almonds

A little off the beaten track to St. Tropez, La Maison des Confitures offers more than 400 different varieties of jam. It really inspires my mum, the queen of jam. She has a knack of going to the Place du Sud market, buying crate-loads of fruit and creating hundreds of flavor combinations. Apricot is our family favorite, but you can use any fruit when it's in season, adjusting the sugar quantity to taste. You'll need a thermometer, a few jam jars and some waxed jar lids (or cut out your own from greaseproof paper).

Halve and pit the apricots, then place them in a saucepan with the sugar over low heat. Bring to a gentle simmer and cook, stirring from time to time, until all the sugar has dissolved. Leave to cool, cover with plastic wrap and allow to settle overnight.

The next day, sterilize the jars. Preheat the oven to 275°F (140°C). Wash the jars carefully using detergent and rinse them well. Place them on a wire rack upside down to drain and put in the oven for 30 minutes. Remove carefully and turn them right side up, being careful not to touch the insides.

Bring the apricots to a boil over a very gentle heat, stirring to prevent the mixture from catching. Using a thermometer, but without letting it touch the bottom of the pan, cook until the jam reaches setting point (220°F/105°C), then simmer for 3-4 minutes more. The top should go frothy and a skin should form. Stir in the almonds and carefully pour the jam into the sterilized jars. Cover with a waxed lid or circle of greaseproof paper that touches the top of the jam. Seal the jars with the lids while the jam is still hot. The jam will keep for 3 months in a cool, dry place and makes a great gift.

CONFITURE DE POIRES À LA VANILLE | PEAR AND VANILLA JAM

MAKES 4 JARS
(8 FL OZ/250 ML EACH)

2 lb (1 kg) ripe pears (about
8 large)
2 vanilla beans
2⅓ cups (19 oz/600 g) jam sugar
juice of 1 lemon

This jam was born to slather over butter on a warm brioche loaf. Try it atop slices of my Ramatuelle Brioche (page 10). I cannot express how ridiculously tasty and good-looking it is!

Peel, quarter, core and finely dice the pears. Split the vanilla beans in half lengthwise and scrape out the seeds with the back of a knife. Put all the ingredients in a saucepan, including the vanilla pods. Cover with plastic wrap and leave to infuse overnight.

The next day, sterilize the jars following the instructions on page 18.

Remove the plastic wrap, place the pears over a gentle heat and bring to a boil, stirring to prevent the mixture from catching. Using a thermometer, but without letting it touch the bottom of the pan, cook until the jam reaches setting point (220°F/105°C). Cook for 3–4 minutes more. Remove from the heat, fish out the vanilla pods and pour the jam into the sterilized jars. Cover with a waxed lid. Seal the jars with the lids while the jam is still hot. Store in a cool, dry place for up to 3 months.

CARAMEL À LA FLEUR DE SEL DE GRIMAUD | SEA-SALTED CARAMEL FROM GRIMAUD

MAKES 2 JARS
(10 FL OZ/300 ML EACH)

1⅓ cups (9½ oz/300 g) unrefined
superfine sugar
1¼ cups (10 fl oz/300 ml)
heavy cream
1 tsp sea salt (you can always
add a little more)

I found my first pot of this caramel when I was wandering around the town of Grimaud at Eastertime, and as soon as the jar was empty I had to have more. It's a fantastic spread for breakfast and makes a delightful sauce for ice cream when warmed. It has become a regular favorite when I sell it from my van, but be warned: I've heard that some jars have had to be confiscated! For an insanely delicious combination, try it with Ramatuelle Brioche (page 10).

Sterilize the jars following the instructions on page 18.

Pour the sugar into a large saucepan and place over medium-high heat. When the sugar begins to melt and turn golden at the edges, give the pan a little shake. Gently swirl the sugar around the pan by tipping the pan from side to side, but do not stir it or the sugar may crystallize. This can take around 10-15 minutes, depending on how hot the pan is.

Cook the caramel until the color begins to darken, then remove from the heat. Slowly and carefully pour in the cream a little at a time, whisking vigorously with a whisk or wooden spoon. The mixture will bubble and steam, but continue mixing until there are no lumps. If there are a few sugar crystals, return the pan to the heat and keep stirring until completely smooth. Now add the sea salt and carefully pour the hot sauce into the sterilized jars. Seal and enjoy once cooled, or store in a cool, dry place for up to 3 months.

CRÊPES DE FESTIVAL À LA FARINE DE CHÂTAIGNE | CHESTNUT FESTIVAL CRÊPES

MAKES 9-10

1²⁄₃ cups (5 oz/150 g) chestnut flour
4 tbsp (2 oz/60 g) unrefined superfine sugar
1 free-range large egg, lightly beaten
1¼ cups (10 fl oz/300 ml) whole milk
2 tsp unsalted butter

I stumbled upon these delightful wafer-thin pancakes during the chestnut festival in Collobrières in late October. They have a delicate, nutty flavor and I particularly love the soft, powdery texture of superfine chestnut flour. They make a healthy breakfast, plus they're gluten-free. For an indulgent treat, try these crêpes with the Chocolate, Hazelnut and Macadamia Spread on page 27.

Mix the chestnut flour, sugar and egg together in a bowl. Continue stirring and drizzle in the milk until it is all incorporated, with no lumps. Place a nonstick frying pan over medium-high heat, add a little butter and move it around to coat the bottom of the pan. Once it has melted, add a small ladle of batter to the pan, quickly swirling it around to create a nice thin crêpe. The crêpes cook faster than normal pancakes, taking just over 1 minute to brown on each side. Before turning it, lift up one side carefully using a slotted spatula to check that the underneath is golden. They are best eaten immediately, but any leftovers can be refrigerated and eaten the next day. The dream would be to slather these in Panna Tierra Chocolate Sauce (page 232), but I tend to go simple and eat them topped with some salted butter or dusted with confectioners' sugar. They're also wonderful with Greek yogurt, honey and fresh strawberries or Sea-Salted Caramel from Grimaud (page 23).

PAUSE POUR PRALINE | HAZELNUT AND ALMOND SPREAD

MAKES 2 JARS
(11 FL OZ/350 ML EACH)

1⅓ cups (6½ oz/200 g) blanched hazelnuts
1¼ cups (6½ oz/200 g) blanched almonds
1¾ cups (13 oz/400 g) unrefined superfine sugar
⅔ cup (5 fl oz/150 ml) water
2 tbsp peanut oil

La Pause Douceur is a beautiful chocolaterie and family business on one of St. Tropez's busiest streets. At Easter it's full to bursting with intricate homemade chocolates and praline. This silky-smooth praline is even better when you have a homemade jar all to yourself.

Sterilize the jars following the instructions on page 18.

Preheat the oven to 400°F (200°C) and prepare a sheet of parchment paper that's about letter size or a little larger. Pour the nuts onto a sheet pan and roast in the oven for about 10 minutes, or until lightly golden, then remove.

To make the caramel, pour the sugar and water into a saucepan and place over medium-high heat. Gently swirl the sugar around the pan by tipping it from side to side, but do not stir it or the sugar may crystallize. Once the caramel is turning golden, remove from the heat and quickly pour in the nuts. Stir with a wooden spoon so that every nut is coated in caramel. Pour onto the prepared parchment paper, spread out the nuts and leave to cool completely for about 1 hour.

Using a knife, break the praline into small pieces and place half of them in a blender. It's usually necessary to stop the machine at least twice and scrape down the sides with a spatula. The mixture will gradually break up, and after 15 minutes the nuts' natural oils will be released and they will begin to form a paste. At this point, drizzle in half of the peanut oil. The mixture should be a little rough, but try to get it as glossy as possible. Pour into a sterilized jar and do the same with the remaining praline. Seal the jars and store in a cool, dry place for up to 1 month.

NINTELLA | CHOCOLATE, HAZELNUT AND MACADAMIA SPREAD

*MAKES 2 JARS
(8 FL OZ/250 ML EACH)*

⅔ cup (3½ oz/100 g)
blanched hazelnuts
⅔ cup (3½ oz/100 g)
macadamia nuts
4 tsp peanut or
sunflower oil
7 tbsp (1¼ oz/40 g) unrefined
superfine sugar
6½ oz (200 g) good-quality
Belgian milk chocolate
2 tbsp (1 oz/30 g) soft unsalted
butter, diced
1 tsp vanilla extract

*Everyone who knows me knows about my little addiction to Nutella.
The problem originated in France: the enormous 1½-pound (750-g) jars
used to be a particular novelty for my sister, Juliana, and me, and there
would be a challenge as to who could scarf the lot first. For this recipe,
you'll need a powerful blender. You can use all hazelnuts if you can't get
ahold of macadamias, and of course you can play around with other
exciting nutty combinations.*

Sterilize the jars following the instructions on page 18.

Preheat the oven to 400°F (200°C). Place the nuts on a
sheet pan and roast for 6–10 minutes, until golden brown.
Carefully tip the hot nuts straight into a blender or food
processor and pulse-blend to break them up, then set to
a high speed and blend until they have formed a paste.
This will take about 10 minutes, and you'll need to stop the
machine at least twice to scrape down the sides and give
the nuts a stir. Gradually drizzle in the peanut oil, then the
sugar, blitzing until the paste becomes silky and fine.

Break the chocolate into a heatproof bowl and set it over
a pan of barely simmering water, making sure the bowl does
not touch the water. Once the chocolate has melted, stir in
the butter and vanilla extract, and then the nut paste. Using
a spatula, scrape into the sterilized jars, seal and store in a
cool, dry place for up to 2 months.

CRÊPES AU BABEURRE, COMPOTE DE CERISES NOIRES ET SIROP D'ÉRABLE | BUTTERMILK PANCAKES WITH BLACK CHERRY COMPOTE AND MAPLE SYRUP

MAKES 10

5 oz (150 g) cherries, the blackest you can find, pitted
1 tbsp unrefined superfine sugar
few drops lemon juice
1 tbsp Grand Marnier
1 cup (5 oz/150 g) all-purpose flour
¼ tsp baking powder
¼ tsp baking soda
½ cup (4 fl oz/120 ml) buttermilk
¼ cup (2 fl oz/60 ml) cold water
1 tsp vanilla extract
3 free-range large eggs, lightly beaten
3½ tbsp (1¾ oz/50 g) unsalted butter, plus extra for serving
1 tsp olive oil
maple syrup, to serve
sea salt

When I think of these buttery, fluffy, golden delights, I want to cook them right away. Topped with cherry compote and maple syrup, these are what dreams are made of.

Put the cherries, sugar and lemon juice in a saucepan over low heat and cook for 5–10 minutes, until the mixture turns into a deep red compote. Add the Grand Marnier, taste and add more sugar if needed. Set aside and keep warm.

For the pancakes, sift together all the dry ingredients along with a pinch of sea salt. In a separate bowl, combine the buttermilk, water and vanilla extract. Slowly stir this mixture into the dry ingredients, then add the beaten eggs. The batter should be lovely and smooth, but don't worry if there's the odd lump.

Melt a little of the butter in a large nonstick frying pan over a medium-high heat. Add 2 separate tablespoons of the mixture to the pan and cook for 1 minute. Use a slotted spatula to make sure the underneath is lovely and golden, then flip the pancakes. Carry on making pancakes, adjusting the temperature if the pan gets too hot and adding more butter and a dash of olive oil to keep the butter from burning. Stack the pancakes on a plate and keep warm. Serve the pancakes in stacks, spooning the black cherry compote on top and around the stack, topping with extra butter and a generous, shameless pour of maple syrup (plus extra once you're halfway down the stack!).

LE GRANOLA DE TONY PARKER | TONY PARKER'S GRANOLA

MAKES ABOUT 2 LB (1 KG)

FOR WHITE GRANOLA
⅓ cup (2 oz/60 g) blanched almonds
½ cup (2¾ oz/80 g) blanched hazelnuts
⅓ cup (2 oz/60 g) raisins
1¼ cups (5 oz/160 g) dried apricots
½ cup (2 oz/60 g) dried cranberries
1 cup (2¾ oz/80 g) unsweetened coconut flakes
3⅓ cups (9½ oz/300 g) rolled oats
4 tsp poppy seeds

FOR GREEN GRANOLA
⅔ cup (2¾ oz/80 g) brazil nuts
½ cup (2¾ oz/80 g) hazelnuts
½ cup (2¾ oz/80 g) dried blueberries
3⅓ cups (9½ oz/300 g) rolled oats
¾ cup plus 2 tbsp (4 oz/120 g) sunflower seeds
scant 1 cup (4 oz/120 g) pumpkin seeds
1 tbsp poppy seeds

FOR THE SYRUP
(enough for one batch of granola)
scant 1 cup (7½ fl oz/220 ml) honey
½ cup (4 fl oz/120 ml) maple syrup
¼ cup (2 fl oz/60 ml) water
¼ cup (2 fl oz/60 ml) sunflower oil
½ tsp salt

When I make this for my dad, Tony, he usually finishes it in about two days. It's supposed to be for breakfast, but he's been known to snack on it six times in one day. Here are my two favorite combinations, which use the same syrup. Feel free to vary the nuts and fruits to create your own combinations. My favorite is the white granola served with coconut milk yogurt, which is hard to beat.

Preheat the oven to 325°F (165°C) and line a sheet pan with parchment paper. Roughly chop up any larger nuts or fruits and toss the nuts, fruits, oats and seeds together in a mixing bowl. Heat all the syrup ingredients in a saucepan and stir well. Pour it over the fruit and nut mixture and tumble the granola together with a wooden spoon until everything is coated in syrup. Tip the mixture onto the sheet pan and push down with the spoon to create a flat layer about ⅜ inch (1 cm) high. Bake for 25 minutes, stirring and breaking up the pieces every 10 minutes until you get lovely golden clusters. Remove and allow to cool completely before storing in an airtight container for up to 3 months.

BROUILLADE AUX LARDONS ET ÉCHALOTES | SCRAMBLED EGGS WITH LARDONS AND SHALLOTS

SERVES 2

3½ oz (100 g) lardons
1 small shallot, thinly sliced
½ tsp superfine sugar
6 free-range large eggs
1 green onion, sliced
1 tsp unsalted butter
1 tbsp olive oil
2 thick slices sourdough bread
sea salt and black pepper

Although I love nothing more than sweet things for breakfast, when I have friends to stay and we've been out in the port the night before, I sometimes need to serve something with a bit more of a kick. These eggs usually do the trick with some grilled sourdough. For those who can hack it, try sprinkling a chopped fresh chile or a pinch of smoked paprika on the eggs. I always keep a sliced sourdough loaf in my freezer so I can enjoy good bread at any time.

Heat a nonstick frying pan over medium-high heat, add the lardons and fry until perfectly crisp, then remove and set aside. In the same pan, add the shallots and sugar and cook until caramelized and golden, then set aside separately.

Preheat the broiler to its highest setting. Break the eggs into a bowl, add the onion, season with salt and pepper and whisk lightly with a fork. Place a saucepan over medium-high heat and, once hot, add the butter and oil. After 1 minute, reduce the heat, add the egg mixture and stir gently with a wooden spoon. (It's best to make scrambled eggs over very low heat so that they form beautiful folds.) Broil the sourdough until lightly toasted. Moments before the eggs are ready, quickly stir in the lardons. Butter the sourdough, then spoon on the shallots and pile on the eggs. Serve *maintenant!*

OMELETTE FAÇON LA MÔLE AUX GIROLLES, GRUYÈRE ET THYM | LA MÔLE-INSPIRED OMELET WITH CHANTERELLES, GRUYÈRE AND THYME

SERVES 2

1 tbsp olive oil
6½ oz (200 g) chanterelle mushrooms
few sprigs fresh thyme
1 large clove garlic, diced
6 free-range large eggs, lightly beaten
3 oz (85 g) Gruyère cheese, finely grated, plus extra for sprinkling
4 tsp unsalted butter
Little Gem lettuce, to serve (optional)
sea salt and black pepper

Just outside St. Tropez, in the town of La Môle, is one of the most intense and overwhelming food experiences to be found in the area: L'Auberge de La Môle, an unassuming bistro with a remarkable quality and quantity of food. One of its classic starters is an omelet, and the last time I was there the chef made one with beautiful golden mushrooms, thyme and Gruyère. I've used chanterelles here, but any other wild or oyster mushrooms would be lovely. You could swap the mushrooms and Gruyère for honey-roast ham and fresh peas, or stuff the omelet with chopped herbs for a fully loaded one from the herb garden.

Heat the oil in a large nonstick frying pan over medium heat, add the chanterelles whole, sprinkle over half the thyme and season with salt and pepper. After a few minutes, add the garlic and stir well. Cook until the mushrooms have shrunk down by half, then remove from the pan and set aside.

Mix the eggs with the grated Gruyère and remaining thyme. In the same frying pan over medium heat, melt half the butter. Pour half the egg mixture into the pan and, using a wooden spoon, swirl it around the pan. As the egg begins to cook and form a layer on the bottom, loosen the omelet with a spatula. Once it is free from the bottom of the pan, start dotting half the mushrooms over one side of the eggs. When the egg on the surface is almost cooked, carefully fold over the mushroom-free side with a spatula to create a half-moon shape. Gently slide the omelet onto a plate and keep warm while making the second one. Serve with some extra cheese on top and crunchy Little Gem lettuce, if you like.

ŒUFS DE CANARD EN COCOTTE ET BRIOCHE GRILLÉE | BAKED DUCK EGGS WITH BRIOCHE FRENCH TOAST

SERVES 2

2 tsp unsalted butter, for greasing
⅓ cup (3 fl oz/80 ml) goat's milk or Greek yogurt
1 tsp olive oil
2 tsp chopped chives, plus extra to serve
freshly grated nutmeg
finely grated zest of ½ unwaxed lemon
2 oz (60 g) smoked salmon, chopped
2 duck eggs
2½ tbsp grated Gruyère cheese
sea salt and black pepper

FOR THE BRIOCHE FRENCH TOAST

2 free-range large chicken eggs
1 tsp ground cinnamon
2 tsp unrefined superfine sugar
1 tbsp whole milk
2 tsp unsalted butter
4 slices brioche

Why have hen's eggs when you can have rich and luxurious duck eggs? Oeufs en cocotte is usually made with crème fraîche or heavy cream, but I prefer using a spoonful of natural Greek or goat's milk yogurt. I admit the brioche French toast is naughty—but it's completely worth it. You could also try swapping the duck egg for two or three quail eggs, depending on how many you can squeeze into the ramekin (note that the quail eggs will take half the cooking time).

Preheat the oven to 350°F (180°C) and lightly butter two ramekins or other small ovenproof pots. In a bowl, mix together all the ingredients except the eggs and Gruyère. Spoon the mixture into the prepared ramekins and carefully crack a duck egg into each one. Season with salt and pepper and sprinkle with Gruyère. Bake for 17–20 minutes, or until a white skin has formed but the egg still wobbles when prodded. The ideal cocotte has a runny yolk that is perfect for dipping.

While the eggs are baking, make the French toast. Whisk the eggs, cinnamon, sugar and milk together and pour half the batter into a shallow bowl. Melt the butter in a frying pan over medium heat. Just as the butter starts to sizzle, dip 2 brioche slices into the eggy batter and coat both sides. Let the excess drip off, then place in the hot pan. After 1–2 minutes, turn the slices over and brown the other sides. Repeat with the rest of the brioche and batter. Serve the cocottes topped with chives alongside the French toast.

LUNCH
DÉJEUNER

DOTTED AROUND THE St. Tropez peninsula, from Brigitte Bardot's house in the bay of Canebiers to the rocky shores of La Moutte and the bay of Pampelonne, are restaurants such as Salins and Graniers and other beach shacks offering tempting, colorful dishes that are perfect for tucking into at lunch when you've just come off the hot beach. These popular haunts have inspired my Driftwood Niçoise Salad and Moules Marinières by Boat. Le Club 55 is also a fantastic hangout; it's not exactly low-key, but it has taught me a lot about the importance of sourcing quality ingredients and fast, fresh cooking. The owner, Patrice de Colmont, and his family have been running this much-loved lunchtime eatery for more than 60 years, and their famous *panier de crudités*, a platter of raw, fantastic-looking vegetables, many of which are grown on their nearby farm, is a feast for the eyes.

After sampling the beach offerings, the next lunch stop is the markets, which are bursting with mouthwatering fresh produce, and I never fail to be inspired by the impressive displays of fish and vegetables. This small area of coastline has many culinary influences, the most prominent of which is Italian. Wood-fired pizzas and pasta dishes can often be found on menus, and although artichokes, eggplants, zucchini and tomatoes are essential in the Italian repertoire, they're also the foundation of many Provençal recipes: try my Artichauts à la Barigoule or Le Mazagran's Ratatouille. I've even traveled as far as Nice to bring you Socca: gluten-free chickpea pancakes, which I serve with cinnamon-roasted carrots and avocado. Other classics from the area are Soupe au Pistou, Pissaladière and Fillet of Sole with Sauce Vierge, all of which are simple, tasty dishes, making lunch a truly memorable event. And I mustn't forget a family favorite, Josh's Steak Tartine, the ultimate sandwich that oozes Saint Agur cheese and juicy caramelized shallots.

LA PISSALADIÈRE DE FÉLINE | THE FÉLINE ONION TART

SERVES 6

2 yellow onions, thinly sliced
1 red onion, thinly sliced
4 small shallots, thinly sliced
2 tbsp olive oil, plus extra to drizzle
1 tsp superfine sugar
1 clove garlic, finely sliced
2 Romano peppers, or 1 red bell pepper
flour, for dusting
½ lb (250 g) fresh or frozen puff pastry (thawed if frozen)
1 free-range large egg yolk, lightly beaten
6–8 anchovy fillets
2½ tsp pitted black olives, chopped
1 tbsp pomegranate molasses
1 tbsp chopped fresh flat-leaf parsley
black pepper

Every year our French neighbors the Félines invite an eclectic crowd to their tranquil secret garden in Port Grimaud. Everyone brings a dish to create a stunning summer buffet. This sweet onion tart, sometimes known as white pizza, is always popular. The recipe is thought to have been introduced to Provence by Roman chefs during the fourteenth-century Avignon Papacy.

Preheat the oven to 400°F (200°C) and line a sheet pan with parchment paper. Put the onions, shallots, olive oil and sugar in a large saucepan over medium heat and cook for 20 minutes without letting them brown. Add the garlic and allow to color for a few minutes.

Meanwhile, roast the peppers whole in the oven for about 20 minutes, until soft. Remove and leave to cool for 5 minutes before peeling off the skin, chopping off the tops and seeding them. Slice into long ⅜-inch (1-cm) wide strips and set aside.

On a lightly floured work surface, roll out the puff pastry into roughly a 15 x 9-inch (38 cm x 23-cm) rectangle and place on the prepared sheet pan. Brush the pastry with the beaten egg yolk and bake for about 15 minutes, until puffed up and golden. Remove and spoon over the onions, leaving a ⅜-inch (1-cm) border. Arrange the pepper strips, anchovies and olives over the top. Drizzle with olive oil and return to the oven for 5 more minutes. Drizzle with the pomegranate molasses, sprinkle with the parsley and season with black pepper. Serve hot or at room temperature.

TARTE À LA BETTE À CARDES ROSES ET AUX LÉGUMES | PINK CHARD AND VEGETABLE TART

SERVES 4

1 eggplant, cut into slices ⅜ inch (1 cm) thick
scant 1 cup (5 oz/150 g) cherry tomatoes, halved
2 tbsp olive oil
pinch of sugar
5–6 leaves pink chard (or use ordinary chard)
1 small radicchio rosso (or use red Belgian endive or chicory), leaves separated
2 cloves garlic, diced
2 tbsp balsamic vinegar
½ lb (250 g) fresh or frozen puff pastry (thawed if frozen)
flour, for dusting
1 free-range large egg yolk, lightly beaten
fresh basil leaves, to serve
1 tbsp extra-virgin olive oil
sea salt and black pepper

I'm constantly thinking up new ways to enjoy eggplants and tomatoes together, and on one outing to the market at La Garde-Freinet I stumbled upon some gorgeous fuchsia-pink chard. The bitterness of the chard and radicchio rosso perfectly complements the sweet tomatoes.

Preheat the oven to 350°F (180°C) and grease and line a 10-inch (25-cm) tart pan with removable bottom with parchment paper. Place the eggplant slices on paper towels and sprinkle with salt. After 10 minutes, pat dry with paper towels. Season with pepper, drizzle with 1 tablespoon olive oil and place on one side of a large sheet pan. Season the tomatoes with salt, pepper and sugar and arrange them, cut side up, on the other side of the sheet pan. Roast for about 20 minutes, until tender, turning the eggplant slices halfway through. The tomatoes may take a little longer; you want them to be shriveled up at the edges.

Meanwhile, slice the chard stalks and roughly chop the radicchio leaves, setting a few whole leaves and sliced stalks aside for garnishing. Heat 1 tablespoon olive oil in a frying pan over medium heat, add the chopped leaves and sliced stalks and cook for 7 minutes, or until wilted by about half. Add the garlic and balsamic vinegar, season with salt and pepper, cook for 2 more minutes, then remove from the heat.

Increase the oven temperature to 400°F (200°C). Roll out the pastry on a lightly floured work surface to fit the prepared tart pan and brush it with the beaten egg yolk. Bake for about 13 minutes, until golden and puffed up, then remove from the pan. Spoon the chard-radicchio mixture onto the pastry, arrange the roasted eggplant and tomatoes on top, add the reserved radicchio leaves and pink chard stalks and scatter over a few basil leaves. Finish with a drizzle of extra-virgin olive oil and serve immediately.

PIZZA D'ELVIS | ELVIS PIZZA

MAKES 5-6 PIZZA BASES

2 tsp fresh yeast
or 1¼ tsp instant yeast
4¼ cups (650 g) extra-fine
00 flour, plus extra for dusting
5 tsp olive oil
3½ tbsp warm milk or water
(if using fresh yeast)
1⅓ cups (325 ml) warm water
4 tsp salt
1 tbsp unrefined superfine sugar
4 tbsp vegetable oil

This is pizza created by the Provençal king himself (pictured overleaf). Selling it out of his old blue truck on the road to St. Maxime, Elvis is usually shirtless, sporting a quiff and blue jeans and listening to rock 'n' roll. I have never tasted pizza this crispy and boasting so much character! Once you've mastered the quick recipe for the pizza base, the combinations of toppings are endless. The toppings should be thin and light, otherwise they won't cook and may spill over.

If using fresh yeast, dissolve it in the 3½ tbsp warm milk or water and set aside for 5 minutes. Mix together all the dry ingredients in a large bowl, make a well and add the olive oil. Combine the milk and the water and pour it slowly into the bowl, stirring constantly. The dough should come together in a ball. Knead the dough on a lightly floured surface for 5 minutes, or until it springs back when pressed with a finger. Place in a bowl, cover with plastic wrap and leave to rise in a warm, dry place for 1½-2 hours, or until it has doubled in size.

Tip the dough out onto the lightly floured work surface and punch it down. Roll it into a ball, place it back in the bowl, cover with plastic wrap and leave to rise in a warm place for another 30 minutes.

Preheat the oven to 425°F (220°C). Line two sheet pans to fit all the pizza bases with parchment paper. Mix together 1 tablespoon flour and the vegetable oil to make a paste and sprinkle it over the pan. Bake in the oven for about 5 minutes, or until the oil and flour have gone brown and smoky. This will give the pizza a wood-fired-tasting base.

Just before rolling out the dough, put the sheet pans back in the oven. Divide the dough into six balls and roll two balls into very thin disks. Carefully pull out the hot sheet pans, place the bases on them, add some of the toppings and cook for 10-15 minutes, lifting the base to check that the underneath is cooked. Repeat with the remaining dough. Serve immediately.

MUSHROOM, GOAT CHEESE AND TARRAGON PIZZA

MAKES ENOUGH TOPPING FOR 5-6 PIZZAS

2 tbsp olive oil
2 shallots, diced
4 cloves garlic, diced
2 cups (12½ oz/400 g) canned chopped tomatoes
2 tsp sugar
good pinch of herbes de Provence
13 oz (400 g) fresh chanterelle or sliced cremini mushrooms
6½ oz (200 g) goat cheese, cut into ⅜-inch (1-cm) pieces
bunch fresh tarragon
4 tbsp extra-virgin olive oil
sea salt and black pepper

Heat the olive oil in a pan over medium heat, add the shallots and cook gently until translucent. Add the garlic and cook for a moment before pouring in the tomatoes, sugar and herbes de Provence; season with salt and pepper. Cook gently for 10–15 minutes, or until the sauce has thickened and reduced by half. Taste and adjust the seasoning if necessary.

Coat the pizza bases with the tomato sauce, leaving a border. Scatter the mushrooms and goat cheese on top and bake as described opposite. Remove from the oven, top with the tarragon, drizzle with extra-virgin olive oil and season with salt and pepper. *E buono!*

ROULOTTE

SALADE NIÇOISE DU BOIS FLOTTÉ | DRIFTWOOD SALAD NIÇOISE

SERVES 2

6½ oz (200 g) Jerusalem artichokes (about 4)
1 tbsp olive oil
2 free-range large eggs
3½ oz (100 g) green beans
6–8 anchovy fillets
1 round head lettuce
½ cup (3½ oz/100 g) cherry tomatoes, halved
1 shallot, diced
⅔ cup (2½ oz/80 g) black olives, pitted and roughly chopped
1 can (6½ oz/200 g) good-quality tuna
sea salt and black pepper

FOR THE DRESSING
3 tbsp extra-virgin olive oil
2 tbsp white wine vinegar
1 tsp whole-grain mustard
finely grated zest and juice of ½ unwaxed lemon
sea salt and black pepper

French salads often feel more vibrant than the lettuce-only affairs back home. Packed with tasty ingredients like lardons, fried mushrooms, grilled zucchini, sun-dried tomatoes and salty croutons, the flavors spill off your plate. My Niçoise salad, inspired by a charming little beach café with driftwood tables and chairs, is no different. Traditionally it's served with new potatoes, but I prefer the texture of roasted Jerusalem artichokes.

Preheat the oven to 350°F (180°C). Quarter the artichokes and put them in a small baking pan. Toss them in olive oil and season with salt and pepper, then roast for about 1 hour, or until soft. Remove and leave to cool.

While the artichokes are roasting, bring a pan of water to a rolling boil. Carefully add the eggs and cook for 3 minutes, then add the beans and cook 6 minutes more. Remove the eggs, then drain the beans and leave to cool. Shell and halve the eggs and roughly chop the anchovies.

Tear the lettuce into a large bowl and add all the ingredients except the eggs and tuna. In a small bowl, mix the dressing ingredients together and taste to check the seasoning. Toss the salad with the dressing, reserving 2 tablespoons for later.

To serve, make a mound of salad in a serving bowl, add the tuna chunks and place the egg halves on top. Drizzle with the remaining dressing. Any leftovers will be perfect in a *pan bagnat*: a hollowed-out French sourdough with the salad packed inside to make a sandwich.

ÉPIS DE MAÏS DE SALINS | SALINS CORN ON THE COB

SERVES 4

4 large ears corn,
or 8 small ones, shucked
4 tbsp olive oil
1 tsp flaky sea salt
1 tsp black pepper
3½ tbsp (1¾ oz/50 g) unsalted
butter
1 clove garlic, diced
2 tbsp chopped fresh
flat-leaf parsley
pinch of cayenne pepper
(optional)

This fantastic buttery corn on the cob is another favorite from the beach bars. Salins, a beach restaurant on the Pampelonne, serves mouthwatering corn that is ideal for when you've just come off the beach. These corn cobs take only minutes to prepare and make an excellent easy lunch. They're even better if you cook them on the barbecue and serve with my sea bass parcels (page 187).

Bring a pan of water to a boil and cook the corn for 10 minutes, or until just tender.

Place a griddle pan over medium-high heat and season the corn generously with olive oil, salt and pepper. Place the corn on the pan and cook, turning as needed, until golden and charred on all sides. The corn should be cooked through after about 6 minutes.

Melt 2 teaspoons of the butter in a frying pan and fry each charred corn ear for about 1 minute, then remove. Wipe out the frying pan, melt the remaining butter and add the garlic. Cook for a few minutes, until golden. Pour the butter and garlic into a small bowl and stir in half the chopped parsley. Sprinkle the corn with the remaining parsley and the cayenne pepper, if using, and serve with the melted garlic butter for drizzling.

TABOULÉ DU GÉANT CASINO | GÉANT CASINO TABBOULEH

SERVES 4 AS A SIDE DISH

⅔ cup (4 oz/120 g) bulgur
2⅓ cups (19 fl oz/600 ml) cold water
⅔ cup (3½ oz/100 g) blanched almonds
large bunch fresh flat-leaf parsley, finely chopped
large bunch fresh mint, finely chopped
3 tomatoes, seeded and diced
finely grated zest and juice of 2 unwaxed lemons
3 carrots, grated
1 red onion, finely diced
2 tsp ground sumac (optional)
3 tbsp extra-virgin olive oil
sea salt and black pepper

This may sound like a rather glamorous salad, but the Géant Casino is actually an enormous, almost overwhelming supermarket jam-packed full of delicious things, including tasty preprepared salads. Here's my version of their tabbouleh—just made for picnic lunches.

Wash the bulgur thoroughly in cold water, then place in a saucepan with the water and bring to a boil. Once bubbling, reduce the heat to a low simmer and cook, covered, for 10 minutes, until most of the water has been soaked up and the bulgur is tender. Drain, if necessary, and set aside.

Meanwhile, place a frying pan over medium-high heat, add the almonds and toast, shaking the pan frequently, until nutty, golden and smoky. Remove and roughly chop them. Put the parsley and mint in a large salad bowl with the rest of the ingredients and toss everything together. Taste and check for seasoning. This will keep well in the fridge for 2 days.

SALADE DE CHÈVRE CHAUD DE LA PLACE DU SUD | PLACE DU SUD WARM GOAT CHEESE SALAD

SERVES 2

⅔ cup (3½ oz/100 g) hazelnuts
1 round head lettuce
2½ cups (1¾ oz/50 g) arugula leaves
4 Black Mission figs, quartered
1 tbsp olive oil
5 oz (150 g) goat cheese

FOR THE DRESSING
2 tsp honey
3 tbsp extra-virgin olive oil
1 tbsp lemon juice
1 tsp chopped fresh thyme leaves
sea salt and black pepper

Just the thought of this salad makes me happy. It reminds me of when my grandmother Bubi would take me to the Place du Sud for one of our lunch dates. It's a five-minute walk over the bridge from our house, and on the way home Bubi would always like to stop and have a time-out with me on the bench at the bottom of the bridge.

Whisk all the dressing ingredients in a bowl and taste to check the seasoning. Heat a saucepan over medium-high heat, add the hazelnuts and toast, shaking the pan, until slightly darker in color. Tip out and leave to cool. Roughly chop about half the nuts, keeping the rest whole. Wash the lettuce and arugula leaves, dry in a salad spinner and tear them into a mixing bowl. Add the figs and hazelnuts.

Add the olive oil to the same pan over medium heat. Cut the cheese into slices ⅜ inch (1 cm) thick, and when the oil is hot, fry the slices for about 1 minute, until golden. Turn over to brown the other side, then remove from the heat and top with 1 tablespoon of the honey dressing. Toss the salad in the rest of the dressing. Carefully arrange a few slices of the warm cheese on the serving plates, followed by a mound of leaves on top. Pile on the nuts and figs and finish with the last of the cheese. Serve immediately.

SIX VINAIGRETTES | SIX DRESSINGS

*EACH MAKES ABOUT
6½ TBSP (3½ FL OZ/100 ML)*

*I tend to use a good-quality extra-virgin olive oil for dressings, but it's
an expensive habit to get into! One with a strong peppery note will add
buckets of flavor and sophistication to your dish. Here are six winners.
Each makes roughly enough dressing for a salad serving four.*

GARLIC

1 large clove garlic
½ tsp sea salt
4 tbsp extra-virgin olive oil
few drops lemon juice
pinch black pepper
pinch sugar

Pound the garlic and salt to a paste with a mortar and pestle. Slowly drizzle
in the olive oil, stirring vigorously, then add the lemon juice, pepper and
sugar. Taste and adjust the seasoning and lemon juice if needed. It keeps
for 3 days in the fridge in a sealed container. It's good with healthy
vegetable salads such as green beans, broccoli and artichokes.

LEMON

3 tbsp extra-virgin olive oil
finely grated zest and juice of
½ unwaxed lemon
pinch sugar
sea salt and black pepper

Shake all the ingredients together in a jam jar, taste to check the seasoning
and serve. It keeps for 3 days in the fridge in a sealed container. To make
a honey-lemon dressing, add ½–1 teaspoon honey. This dressing is amazing
in a salad of avocado and leftover chicken.

HONEY-MUSTARD

1 tsp whole-grain mustard
4 tbsp extra-virgin olive oil
finely grated zest and juice of
½ unwaxed lemon
1 tsp honey
sea salt and black pepper

Shake everything together in a jam jar, taste to check the seasoning and
serve. It keeps for 4 days in the fridge in a sealed container. This is a great
little number to mix through a cold potato, lardon and chive salad.

BALSAMIC

3 tbsp extra-virgin olive oil
2 tbsp balsamic vinegar
½ clove garlic, diced
sea salt and black pepper

Shake everything together in a jam jar, taste to check the seasoning and serve. It keeps for 3 days in the fridge in a sealed container, or for 1 week if you leave out the garlic. This salad dressing goes particularly well with the Tomato, Mozzarella and Crouton Salad (page 70).

TARRAGON

¼ tsp chopped garlic
2 tbsp chopped fresh
tarragon leaves
4 tbsp extra-virgin olive oil
2 tsp cider vinegar
2 tsp lemon juice
¼ tsp sugar
sea salt and black pepper

Pound the garlic and a little salt to a paste with a mortar and pestle. Add the rest of the ingredients and taste to check for seasoning. This dressing keeps for 3 days in the fridge in a sealed container, and is just made for chicken and avocado salads.

MERLOT

3 tbsp extra-virgin olive oil
2 tbsp Merlot vinegar
½–1 tsp runny honey,
according to taste
sea salt and black pepper

Shake all the ingredients together in a jam jar. Taste to check the seasoning. Done! In my opinion, this one wins the race. Invest in the glossy, velvety nectar otherwise known as Merlot vinegar. Made from Spanish Merlot wine, where the grapes are aged in barrels made from French oak, it develops berry aromas and clear vanilla notes. The latter is perhaps why I can't get enough of it. I scatter it over all kinds of things, from raw tuna to grilled lobster to eggplant caviar. It's magical! The dressing keeps for 1 week in the fridge in a sealed container.

SOCCA DE NICE, AVOCAT ÉCRASÉ, CAROTTES RÔTIES

SOCCA FROM NICE WITH CRUSHED AVOCADO, ROASTED CARROTS

SERVES 3

3 large carrots
4 tsp avocado oil, plus extra
for cooking socca
½ tsp ground cinnamon
1 cup (3 oz/90 g) chickpea flour
(also known as gram flour)
½ cup plus 1 tbsp (4½ fl oz/140 ml)
cold water
1 tsp chopped fresh rosemary
1 tsp pumpkin seeds
1 tsp sunflower seeds
finely grated zest of ½ unwaxed
lemon, plus 1 tbsp juice
2 ripe avocados
2 tbsp chopped fresh chives
sea salt and black pepper

FOR THE DRESSING
3 tbsp goat's milk or Greek yogurt
2 tbsp extra-virgin olive oil
finely grated zest and juice of
½ unwaxed lemon
sea salt and black pepper

Socca are rather charming and unusual pancakes made with chickpea flour. They're super-healthy, wheat- and gluten-free, and fantastic for lunch. You can also make them into pizzette by topping them with tomatoes and cheese, then grilling them.

Preheat the oven to 400°F (200°C). Slice the carrots lengthwise into thin strips, season with salt and pepper, sprinkle with a little avocado oil and cinnamon and spread on a sheet pan. Roast for about 40 minutes, until tender and golden.

Meanwhile, mix the chickpea flour, cold water, rosemary, pumpkin and sunflower seeds and lemon zest in a bowl and add a few drops of lemon juice. Leave to stand for 15 minutes. In the meantime, whisk all the dressing ingredients together, taste to check the seasoning and set aside in the fridge. Halve, peel, pit and lightly mash the avocados in a separate bowl, leaving some chunks. Season with salt and pepper and add the remaining lemon juice, a splash of avocado oil and the chives.

Start cooking the socca when the carrots are almost ready. Heat 1 tablespoon avocado oil in a frying pan over medium heat and pour in a little of the batter. After about 1 minute the underneath should be golden; flip the pancake over with a spatula. Cook for another minute or so, then remove and repeat with the remaining batter. Arrange the socca on three plates with a generous spoonful of the crushed avocado and a few cinnamon-roasted carrots, then drizzle with the yogurt dressing. Serve immediately.

SOUPE AU PISTOU | SOUP WITH PISTOU

SERVES 4

2 tbsp olive oil
2 banana shallots or 5-6 regular shallots, diced
½ leek, finely chopped
2 cloves garlic, diced
2 carrots, diced
3 new potatoes or 1 large potato, diced
3½ oz (100 g) tomatoes, chopped
4 cups (32 fl oz/1 l) water
1 tsp superfine sugar
1 cup (6½ oz/200 g) rinsed and drained canned chickpeas
3½ oz (100 g) green beans, cut into ¾-inch (2-cm) pieces
⅔ cup (3½ oz/100 g) fresh or frozen peas
2 tbsp chopped fresh flat-leaf parsley
finely grated zest and juice of 2 unwaxed lemons
3½ oz (100 g) Gruyère cheese, grated (optional)
2 tbsp extra-virgin olive oil
sea salt and black pepper

FOR THE PISTOU
(makes more than you'll need for the soup)
4 cloves garlic
½ tsp sea salt
large bunch fresh basil, chopped
few drops lemon juice
2-3 tbsp extra-virgin olive oil
2 tbsp grated Gruyère cheese
black pepper

This summer soup is an iconic Provençal dish made with cubed vegetables and a dollop of pistou on top. Pistou means "pounded" in the Provençal language and is simply made with garlic, fresh basil and olive oil—like pesto. There are many Italian influences on the local cuisine because 30 percent of the population are Italian in origin.

Make the pistou. Using a mortar and pestle, pound the garlic and salt to a paste. Add the chopped basil and lemon juice and stir. (Lemon juice prevents the basil from going black and helps retain its color.) Stir in the olive oil, season with black pepper and mix in the Gruyère. If you don't have a large mortar and pestle, finely chop the garlic, sprinkle over the salt and squash them together on a chopping board with the side of a knife until they form a paste. Put the garlic paste in a bowl and stir in the chopped basil and lemon juice, then add the olive oil and black pepper, and finally add the grated Gruyère. Taste to check the seasoning. This will keep in the fridge for 3 days.

Prepare and chop all the vegetables before starting to cook. Heat the olive oil in a large saucepan over medium heat, then add the shallots and leek. Cook until translucent, then add the garlic and cook for a moment longer. Stir in the carrots, potatoes and tomatoes and let the flavors infuse before adding the water and sugar, and seasoning with salt and pepper. Bring the water to a boil and then reduce the heat to a simmer. Cook for 15-20 minutes, until the vegetables are tender but still have a little bite to them.

Once the vegetables are almost tender, stir in the chickpeas and green beans and simmer for 5 minutes. Add the peas, parsley, lemon zest and juice and half the Gruyère, if using. Stir well, taste and check the seasoning. Cook for 2 minutes longer, until the peas are just tender. Serve in bowls with a teaspoon of pistou on top, a little more Gruyère, if you like, and a drizzle of extra-virgin olive oil.

RATATOUILLE DU MAZAGRAN | LE MAZAGRAN'S RATATOUILLE

SERVES 6

1 tbsp olive oil, plus extra for drizzling
2 banana shallots or 5–6 regular shallots, diced
large bunch fresh basil
4 cloves garlic, very thinly sliced
4 tsp unsalted butter
4 zucchini, sliced ¼ inch (5 mm) thick
1 can (28 oz/875 g) plum tomatoes
2 eggplants, sliced ⅜ inch (1 cm) thick
1 butternut squash, peeled, seeded and roughly chopped
2¼ cups (13 oz/400 g) cherry tomatoes, halved
2 tsp paprika
sea salt and black pepper

A wonderful local restaurant, Le Mazagran, makes a beautiful, rich, slow-cooked ratatouille that's full of summer flavors. It tastes even better the day after you make it. I like it for lunch with couscous or brown rice (or try it with Socca, page 60), but it's particularly St. Tropez-style served as a side with white fish and frites. Make it in summer, when the vegetables are at their absolute best.

Heat a little olive oil in a pan over medium-high heat, add the shallots and cook until translucent. Cut the stems off the basil, finely chop them and add to the pan. Once the basil stems have softened, add the garlic and cook for 1 minute. Add the butter and zucchini, stirring well, then add the tomatoes and 1¼ cups (10 fl oz/300 ml) water. Bring to a boil, then reduce the heat to a low simmer and cook for 1½ hours to thicken and reduce. Taste and season with some salt and pepper.

Meanwhile, preheat the oven to 400°F (200°C). Line two sheet pans with parchment paper. Place the eggplant slices in a colander and sprinkle with salt. Set aside for 10 minutes and pat dry with paper towels. Put the eggplant and squash on one sheet pan, keeping them apart, and the cherry tomatoes on the other. Season with salt and pepper and drizzle with olive oil. Toss the squash in the paprika. Roast the tomatoes for 20–30 minutes, or until shriveled and sweet. Roast the eggplant and squash for about 40 minutes, or until soft and golden.

Once the sauce has simmered, add the roasted vegetables to the pan along with the cherry tomatoes. Roughly tear the basil leaves and toss them into the ratatouille just before serving. Taste and adjust the seasoning if needed. This is still fantastic a couple of days later.

ARTICHAUTS À LA BARIGOULE | ARTICHOKE HEARTS IN OLIVE OIL

SERVES 4

finely grated zest and juice
of 1 unwaxed lemon,
plus 4 thin slices
4 medium artichokes
⅔ cup (5 fl oz/150 ml) olive oil
10 oz (300 g) cremini mushrooms
4 small carrots, quartered
lengthwise
6 cloves garlic, crushed
⅔ cup (5 fl oz/150 ml) white wine
1 handful fresh flat-leaf parsley,
roughly chopped
6 black olives, pitted
baguette and green salad leaves,
to serve
sea salt and black pepper

Artichokes always remind me of the south of France because they appear in so many dishes there. I remember eating my first whole one, peeling back the layers and dipping them in a rich, creamy mayonnaise sauce. These taste incredible because they've been completely drenched in olive oil, lemon and white wine, and have had time to soak up the flavors. Don't use your most expensive olive oil for this one! You can prepare this dish a day in advance.

Mix the lemon juice with 6 cups (48 fl oz/1.5 l) water in a large bowl. One by one, cut off the outer leaves of the artichokes until you get to the yellow leaves. Using a vegetable peeler, remove any outer green layer from the stem and trim off about half of the stem. Use a spoon to carefully scoop out and discard the fuzzy center (the choke), quarter the artichoke and place in the lemon water while you get on with the others.

Drain the artichokes. Heat the oil in a large saucepan over medium-high heat. Add the artichokes, cut sides down, along with the mushrooms, carrots and garlic. Cook, stirring constantly, for about 10 minutes, or until the vegetables begin to brown. Add the lemon slices and wine, bring to a boil and reduce by half. Pour over enough water to just cover the vegetables and reduce the heat to a simmer. Cook for another 10 minutes, until the vegetables are tender.

Using tongs, remove the carrots, mushrooms and artichokes and turn up the heat to reduce the liquid by about one-third. This will take another 10 minutes. Return the vegetables to the sauce to heat through, then season with salt and pepper. Garnish with the lemon zest, parsley and olives. Serve scattered over serving plates with drops of the sauce drizzled among them, with a fresh baguette and green salad.

SALADE DE TOMATES À LA MOZZARELLA ET AUX CROÛTONS | TOMATO, MOZZARELLA AND CROUTON SALAD

SERVES 2

3½ oz (100 g) stale baguette or sourdough
1 tbsp olive oil
1 rounded cup (6½ oz/200 g) cherry tomatoes, halved
6½ oz (200 g) heirloom or plum tomatoes, thinly sliced
1 small shallot, thinly sliced
small bunch fresh basil
2 balls buffalo mozzarella, about 200g (6½ oz)
sea salt and black pepper

FOR THE DRESSING
2 tbsp balsamic vinegar
3 tbsp extra-virgin olive oil
½ tsp superfine sugar
sea salt and black pepper

Although it's a classically Italian combination, tomato, mozzarella and basil salad is very common on the south coast of France. The tomatoes there are some of the fattest and juiciest I've ever seen: bursting with so much flavor that they don't really need a dressing. I've added salty croutons to the mix, which is a great way to use up any stale bread. If you can't find heirloom or plum tomatoes, good-quality beefsteak tomatoes will do.

Preheat the oven to 400°F (200°C). Slice the baguette or sourdough into large pieces, season with salt and pepper and drizzle with olive oil. Bake for 5–6 minutes, or until crisp and golden. Remove and set aside to cool.

Mix the dressing ingredients together in a bowl with salt and pepper and taste to check the seasoning. Put all the salad ingredients except the mozzarella and a few basil leaves in a large bowl and gently stir everything together with two-thirds of the dressing. Divide the tomato salad between two serving plates. Roughly tear the mozzarella into six pieces and arrange it on top of and around the tomatoes, scatter the remaining basil leaves on top and drizzle the remaining dressing over the mozzarella and around the plate. *Et voilà!*

COURGE BUTTERNUT RÔTIE ET GRAINES DE FENOUIL SAUVAGE | ROASTED BUTTERNUT SQUASH WITH WILD FENNEL SEEDS

SERVES 3 AS A SIDE DISH

1 large butternut squash
4 tbsp olive oil
2 tsp fennel seeds
1 ball buffalo mozzarella
or burrata cheese,
about ¼ lb/125 g (optional)
sea salt and black pepper

Fennel grows on the roadside pretty much everywhere around St. Tropez. My usual foraging patch is on the way to one of the clothes markets. This dish is really simple and tasty and full of texture and flavor. Best of all, there's absolutely no waste. I usually make it for a healthy weekday lunch and eat it with a fresh green salad.

Preheat the oven to 400°F (200°C) and line two baking pans with parchment paper. Top and tail the squash, then peel the skin off in long strips and reserve it. Halve the squash horizontally and cut the top section into long, steak fry-like chunks. Cut the rest in half down the middle and scoop out the pulp and discard, reserving the seeds. Cut the flesh into similar-sized pieces. Arrange the squash chunks on one baking pan and the skins and seeds on the other. Season with salt and pepper, drizzle with 3 tablespoons of the olive oil and scatter with the fennel seeds. Roast for 18-20 minutes, by which time the skins and seeds should be golden and crisp. Roast the squash for another 30-35 minutes, until golden and tender when poked with a knife. Spoon the roasted squash into a serving bowl and place the seeds and crispy skins on top. Tear the mozzarella or burrata, if using, into pieces and scatter on top. Drizzle with the remaining olive oil and sprinkle with sea salt. Serve warm or cold.

DUO D'ASPERGES HARICOTS VERTS ET VINAIGRETTE AUX NOIX GRILLÉES

ASPARAGUS AND GREEN BEANS IN VINAIGRETTE WITH TOASTED WALNUTS

SERVES 4 AS A SIDE DISH

scant 1 cup (3½ oz/100 g) walnuts
6½ oz (200 g) green beans
6½ oz (200 g) asparagus
sea salt and black pepper

FOR THE DRESSING
1 large clove garlic
4 tbsp peanut oil
2 tbsp white wine vinegar
½ tsp superfine sugar

This is a particular favorite side salad of mine: a wonderful mixture of asparagus and green beans blanched so that they still hold some crunch. Be aware, I am a little addicted to nuts in every salad dish, especially if the nuts in question are toasted!

Preheat the oven to 400°F (200°C). Put the walnuts on a sheet pan and roast for 10-12 minutes, until golden. Transfer to a cutting board and leave to cool, then roughly chop them, leaving a few nuts whole. In the meantime, bring a large saucepan of water to a boil and add 1 teaspoon salt. Trim the beans and asparagus and blanch for about 4 minutes, until tender but still with a little crunch. Drain and leave to cool.

For the dressing, put the garlic and a good pinch of salt into a mortar and mash to a paste with a pestle (or use the back of a knife to squash the garlic and salt together on a cutting board to make a paste, then transfer to a bowl). Whisk in the peanut oil, followed by the rest of the dressing ingredients with some salt and pepper. Taste to check the seasoning. Put the beans, asparagus and nuts in a large serving bowl and toss with the dressing. Taste one last time, then serve warm or cold.

CAROTTES RÂPÉES À LA CORIANDRE ET AUX GRAINES | GRATED CARROTS WITH CILANTRO AND SEEDS

SERVES 2

6½ oz (200 g) carrots (about 5)
bunch fresh cilantro
2 tbsp sunflower seeds
1 tsp poppy seeds

FOR THE DRESSING
2 tbsp white wine vinegar
3 tbsp extra-virgin olive oil
2 tbsp lemon juice
sea salt and black pepper

This healthy French classic always featured in my lunch box when I was doing work experience placements in the local restaurants, to make a change from staff lunch. It's ideal for a picnic because you can dress it before you leave and the carrots never go soggy. For an injection of color and sweetness, you could finely grate in some beets.

Mix together all the dressing ingredients, season with salt and pepper and set aside. Top and tail the carrots, then grate them and place in a serving bowl. Roughly chop the cilantro, add to the bowl along with the seeds and toss with the dressing. Taste to check the seasoning and serve.

GALETTES DE CRABE ET SALADE D'AVOCAT, TOMATE ET CORIANDRE | CRAB CAKES WITH AVOCADO, TOMATO AND CILANTRO SALAD

MAKES 8

1 tbsp pine nuts
2 tsp fennel seeds
10 oz (300 g) crabmeat
5 oz (150 g) peeled, boiled
potatoes (about 2 medium ones)
bunch fresh chives,
finely chopped
3 tbsp olive oil
¾ cup (4 oz/120 g)
all-purpose flour
3 free-range large eggs,
lightly beaten
1 cup (4 oz/120 g) dried
bread crumbs
sea salt and black pepper

FOR THE SALAD
3 large ripe avocados, peeled,
pitted and roughly chopped
1¼ cups (6½ oz/200 g) cherry
tomatoes, quartered
1 banana shallot or 2-3 regular
shallots, diced
large bunch fresh cilantro,
roughly chopped, plus extra
leaves to garnish
2 green onions, chopped
3 tbsp extra-virgin olive oil
2 tbsp white wine vinegar
finely grated zest and juice of
2 limes, plus extra lime for serving
pinch sugar
sea salt and black pepper

I have a funny relationship with crab. When I was 13, I bought a live one from the Géant supermarket because I felt sorry for it, then returned it to the sea under some rocks. Years later, when I was a chef at L'Anima in London, one of my first tasks was to boil six live crabs three times a week. When I dropped the first one into the water, whispering an apology, one of the Italian chefs, Lello, said, "Ey Nina, now you're a killa!" After the fourth one splashed in, he laughed and said, "Ey, now you're a serial killa!" After that experience I started to cook with crab all the time. These crab cakes are perfect for a dinner party.

Prepare the salad ingredients first so you can just toss them all together quickly at the end.

Place a large frying pan over medium-high heat, add the pine nuts and fennel seeds and toast gently for 2 minutes, shaking the pan to color them evenly. Place in a large bowl with the crabmeat, potatoes, chives and 1 tablespoon of the olive oil. Season with salt and pepper and mash it all together. Shape the mixture into eight patties and place on a sheet of parchment paper. Line up three plates with the flour, beaten eggs and bread crumbs, respectively. Coat a patty in the flour, dusting off any excess, then dip in the egg and allow the excess to drip off, then roll it in the bread crumbs and return to the parchment paper. Repeat with all the patties.

Return the large frying pan to medium-high heat and add the remaining olive oil. Fry the crab cakes for about 1-2 minutes, then turn them over. Continue cooking and turning for 6 minutes, until beautifully golden and crisp.

Toss together all the salad ingredients and taste to check the seasoning. Serve immediately, garnishing with extra cilantro leaves and an extra squeeze of lime juice.

NEMS DES GRANIERS | GRANIERS SPRING ROLLS

MAKES 6

FOR THE DIPPING SAUCE
¾ cup plus 1 tbsp (6½ fl oz/
200 ml) white wine vinegar
or rice vinegar
¼ cup (2 oz/60 g) unrefined
superfine sugar
1 tsp salt
½ fresh red chile, seeded
(optional) and chopped

FOR THE ROLLS
½ cucumber, seeds scooped
out, sliced into thin
4-inch (10-cm) sticks
1 large carrot, sliced
into thin sticks
2 green onions, thinly sliced
8 sheets rice paper
3 cups (3½ oz/100 g) baby
spinach leaves
½ lb (250 g) cooked shrimp
6½ oz (200 g) bean sprouts
bunch fresh chives, chopped
bunch fresh cilantro, chopped
2 limes, quartered
½ head Chinese cabbage

Perhaps surprisingly, spring rolls can be found on many of the beach menus. The rolls at the rustic beach shack Les Graniers are a real winner for me: large, tightly packed bundles of crunchy green freshness served on Chinese cabbage leaves. Great for dipping! What's more, they're raw, which means they're healthier than the ones you'll find in Chinese restaurants. They make a lovely light lunch with a salad, or you could make small ones for a party.

For the dipping sauce, heat the vinegar in a saucepan and add the sugar. Once it has dissolved, remove and leave to cool. Add the salt and chile, and it's ready for dipping.

Arrange the sliced vegetables in separate piles on a plate. Place a sheet of rice paper on a work surface and put a spinach leaf on the top third of the sheet, spreading it out flat. Place 3 or more leaves directly underneath the first. These make a guideline for where the fillings will go. Put a few shrimp on the spinach leaves, a few sticks of cucumber and carrot, green onions, bean sprouts and a sprinkle of chives and cilantro, and then finish with a squeeze of lime juice. Wet the edges of the rice sheet with a little water. Fold the bottom of the sheet upward, tucking it in around the filling, then fold the side closest to the ingredients inward, tightly wrapping it around, being sure to tuck the edge under the greens to create a round shape. Continue rolling toward the other end, dabbing with a little more water to make it snug and secure. Make the remaining rolls in the same way. Lastly, carefully pull away the leaves from the Chinese cabbage and arrange them on a serving plate. Sit the spring rolls in the cabbage leaves and wrap the leaves around the rolls like a blanket. Serve with the dipping sauce.

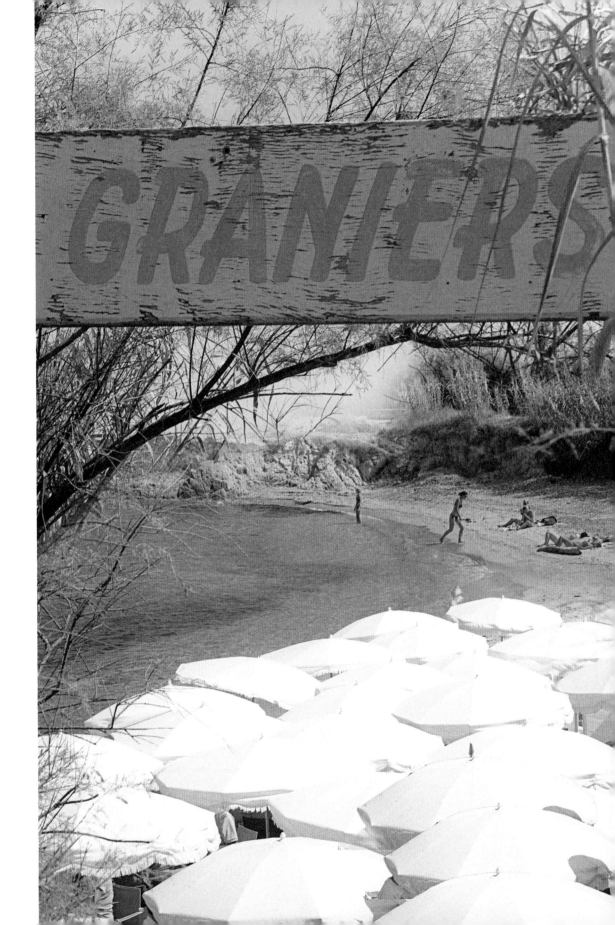

BROCHETTES DE SAINT-JACQUES ET CHORIZO AU THYM | SCALLOP SKEWERS WITH CHORIZO AND THYME

SERVES 4

¾ lb (350 g) scallops,
roe removed, if attached
3½ oz (100 g) soft cooking chorizo
bunch fresh thyme,
leaves roughly chopped
5 tbsp olive oil
scant 1 cup (5 oz/150 g)
cherry tomatoes
2 lemons, halved
4 tsp unsalted butter
sea salt and black pepper

Brochette de Saint-Jacques *is typical of the south of France, and I've added my beloved blood-red Spanish chorizo to the format. You'll need sixteen 5-inch (12-cm) skewers; if you prefer longer skewers, just make sure they fit in the pan. You can keep the scallop roe on if you like, but it's easier to cook the scallops without it.*

Carefully rinse the scallops under cold running water and pat them dry with paper towels. Slice the chorizo into chunks roughly the same size as the scallops. Put the scallops, chorizo and half the thyme in a bowl with some of the olive oil, season with salt and pepper and gently tumble together with your hands, making sure everything is coated.

Thread the scallops, chorizo and tomatoes onto the skewers and sprinkle with the remaining thyme. Heat the remaining oil in two large frying pans over medium-high heat. When the oil is hot, add the skewers and cook for 4–5 minutes, turning every so often, until all sides are browned. One minute before they're ready, squeeze ½ lemon over each. Carefully stack the skewers on a serving dish. Reduce the heat and add the other half of the lemon to each pan. Use a wooden spoon to scrape up all the juices on the bottom of the pans and add half the butter to each pan. Cook for a moment, stirring, before drizzling the tasty pink sauce over the skewers.

MOULES MARINIÈRES EN BATEAU | MOULES MARINIÈRES BY BOAT

SERVES 2

1¼ lb (600 g) mussels, cleaned
4 tsp unsalted butter
2 cloves garlic, diced
2 shallots, diced
1 bouquet garni
6½ tbsp (3½ fl oz/100 ml)
pear cider or dry white wine
2 tbsp crème fraîche
4 tomatoes, seeded and diced
2 tbsp chopped fresh
flat-leaf parsley
2 tbsp chopped fresh cilantro
sea salt and black pepper

Whenever I'm lucky enough to go out fishing with my neighbor Pilou on his boat, I love to cook him something tasty but simple for lunch. Mussels are abundant in the bay of St. Tropez, so they often feature on the plat du jour. It's traditional to use dry white wine, but I use pear cider, which gives the sauce a beautiful fruity sweetness. It's great with tagliatelle if you want something more substantial.

Rinse the mussels well under plenty of cold running water and pull off any of the tough bits of moss or seaweed. They should all be closed; discard any that don't close when tapped sharply on the work surface.

Melt the butter in a large pan, add the garlic and shallots and cook for a few minutes until softened, then add the bouquet garni. Increase the heat and add the mussels and cider or wine and let it all sizzle. Cook, covered, for 4 minutes, shaking the pan from time to time. The mussels should have now opened; discard any that haven't. Remove and discard the bouquet garni and stir in the crème fraîche and diced tomatoes. Remove from the heat, add the chopped herbs, season with salt and pepper and serve. Boom!

FILET DE SOLE À LA SAUCE VIERGE | FILLET OF SOLE WITH SAUCE VIERGE

SERVES 4

½ tsp unsalted butter
1 tbsp olive oil
1 clove garlic, finely sliced
4 sole fillets
juice of 1 lemon, plus
extra to serve
sea salt and black pepper

FOR THE SAUCE VIERGE
1 or 2 green onions, thinly sliced
2 shallots, very finely chopped
bunch fresh chives, finely chopped
1 clove garlic, diced
3 tbsp finely chopped fresh
flat-leaf parsley
10 oz (300 g) tomatoes
(about 4 medium)
4–5 tbsp white wine vinegar
2 tsp unrefined superfine sugar
juice of ½ lemon
4 tbsp (2 fl oz/60 ml) olive oil
sea salt and black pepper

This is a really impressive and quick dish that takes me straight back to the beach—it captures the very essence of St. Tropez flavors. Flatfish like sole are great because the cooking time is a matter of minutes, but I also sometimes use plaice (flounder) or pollack. I usually serve it with a simple green or mixed bean salad, but for a more substantial lunch, it's great with garlicky roast potatoes and peppers. The sauce is also delicious with pasta, or as a salad dressing.

First, make the sauce. Put the green onions, shallots, chives, garlic and parsley in a bowl. Halve, quarter and seed the tomatoes, discarding any liquid. Pat them dry with paper towels and slice them into long strips, then finely dice and add to the bowl. Stir in the rest of the ingredients and taste to check the seasoning. It should taste sharp and a little acidic, but with a hint of sweetness.

Next, heat the butter and olive oil in a large frying pan over medium-high heat until it sizzles, then add the garlic. Reduce the heat to medium, add the fillets, skin side down, and cook for 3–4 minutes. Squeeze the lemon juice over the fish, carefully turn over the fillets and cook for 1–2 minutes more, until they start to flake away gently. Serve immediately topped with the sauce vierge and an extra squeeze of lemon.

POULET DU BUN MAN | BUN MAN CHICKEN

SERVES 4–5

1 whole chicken, 3 lb (1.5 kg)
2 whole heads garlic, cloves peeled and roughly crushed
1 red onion, roughly chopped
2 lemons, halved
bunch fresh rosemary
3 tbsp olive oil
1 tsp paprika
½ tsp ground turmeric
½ tsp ground cumin
sea salt and black pepper

Ever since I was little, there has been a butcher's stall near my house run by a fascinating man called the Bun Man. His hair is tied in a bun on the crown of his head, he wears mascara, he walks in clogs with a limp and he has a pet goose in a basket next to his stall. When I buy one of his chickens I can only make one roast, and this is it.

Preheat the oven to 350°F (180°C) and place the chicken in a roasting pan. Using a sharp knife, carefully make a few incisions through the skin over the breast and legs of the bird. Do not cut into the flesh. Gently push your finger through the cuts to make a hole under the skin and push a piece of garlic into each gap. Put a handful of red onion inside the cavity along with 3 lemon halves, the rosemary and any leftover garlic. Arrange the remaining red onion under the chicken, finely slice the last lemon half and arrange the pieces around the bird. Mix together the olive oil and spices to make a paste and cover the chicken with it. Season with salt and pepper and roast in the oven for 40 minutes before turning it upside down and roasting for another 25 minutes. Turn it right side up again and cook for 10–15 minutes more. To check if the chicken is cooked, gently tug at one of the legs; it will break away effortlessly when ready. Allow it to rest for a few minutes before serving with Aïoli.

AÏOLI

MAKES ABOUT 1⅔ CUPS (13 FL OZ/400 ML)

1 free-range large egg yolk
about 1¼ cups (10 fl oz/300 ml) sunflower oil
3–4 cloves garlic, roasted and crushed
1 tbsp white wine vinegar
pinch of sugar
finely grated lemon zest and a few drops juice
sea salt and black pepper

When I'm roasting a chicken, I chuck in a few garlic cloves for the last 30 minutes and let them roast until sweet and sticky. This can be mixed with any flavor you like. Try it with fresh herbs, raw garlic or smoked paprika, saffron or harissa.

Whisk the egg yolk with an electric handheld beater or balloon whisk. Very slowly, drizzle in a little sunflower oil while whisking, then continue until it's all incorporated. This will take a few minutes of constant whisking. The yolk will become pale and shiny. Add the oil very slowly or the mayonnaise will not emulsify. Add the garlic, vinegar, sugar, lemon juice and zest to taste. Add any other flavorings, if using, and season with salt and pepper.

TARTINE DE STEAK DE JOSH AU SAINT AGUR ET AUX ÉCHALOTES CARAMÉLISÉES | JOSH'S STEAK TARTINE WITH SAINT AGUR AND CARAMELIZED SHALLOTS

SERVES 4

3 tbsp olive oil
3 small shallots, thinly sliced
1 tsp sugar
1 large sirloin steak,
about 7 oz (200 g)
1 tbsp peanut oil
4 slices sourdough
1 small clove garlic, halved
2½ tbsp crumbled Saint Agur
cheese (or another blue cheese,
such as Roquefort)
⅔ cup (¾ oz/20 g) arugula leaves
(optional)
sea salt and black pepper

FOR THE DRESSING
3 tbsp extra-virgin olive oil
2 tbsp Merlot vinegar or
balsamic vinegar
sea salt and black pepper

My brother-in-law Josh is really into his sandwiches and considers himself a pretty good sandwich maker. This bad-boy tartine tower rivals a BLT or chicken club any day of the week. It's sandwich heaven . . . do it!

Preheat the broiler. Heat 2 tablespoons of the oil in a small frying pan, add the shallots and sugar and cook over medium-low heat for 10 minutes, until soft and caramelized. Place a frying pan over high heat, season the steak well with salt and pepper and drizzle with the remaining olive oil. Add the peanut oil to the pan and let it heat for a moment before adding the steak. Fry for 2 minutes, then turn over and cook for another 3 minutes for rare, 3½ minutes for medium-rare, or 4 minutes for medium (the exact timings will depend on the thickness). Remove, reserving any juices, and leave to rest for 7 minutes.

While the steak is resting, toast the bread under the broiler and immediately rub with the garlic clove. While the bread is still hot, scatter half the blue cheese on top, pressing it into the slices, and sprinkle with some shallots. Cut the steak lengthwise into chunks (about 8 pieces) and place them on top of the shallots. Mix together all the dressing ingredients in a small bowl, including any meat juices. Top the steak with the remaining shallots and blue cheese. If using, pile the arugula over the steak and drizzle the dressing over the tartines. Serve immediately.

TEATIME
GOÛTER

BEHIND THE PORT'S iconic pastel-colored facades are a number of expert delicatessens and chocolatiers. They work like crazy to fill their displays with treats like the glossy, burnt caramel apricot tarts, dark *moelleux au chocolat*, tortes and puff pastries toppling over with vanilla cream and Armagnac-soaked cherries. One concoction in particular is a clear favorite, and my sister Juliana and I have been addicted to it for many years: Tarte Tropézienne. It's more like a cake than a tart, a delightfully sweet brioche filled with a delicate almond *crème pâtissière*. These days it is sold all over the region, but the undeniably winning version is found at the Sénéquier bakery, where the recipe is a closely guarded secret. When you walk in, and once the heavenly smell of freshly baked bread has subsided, you become aware of Sénéquier's other secret weapon: nougat, wrapped beautifully in silver foil. This wonderfully soft, gooey sweet is crammed with lightly toasted pistachios

and almonds and has a delicate orange blossom aftertaste. It has taken me many attempts to get the consistency just right. This was another trade secret that the bakery boys would not give up, but it's well worth trying for a slightly more challenging sweet treat.

I grew up in a family of teatime lovers and tart makers, so it is possible that my fondness for cakes and sugar might be a little excessive. My mother's simple apricot tart is a permanent temptation in the kitchen. I am always looking to local ingredients for inspiration, such as the rose water from the Pampelonne rose farm, nuts from the almond trees in Grimaud, and even homegrown white peaches from a roadside stall on the way to Gassin, which was the inspiration behind my White Chocolate Tart with Amaretto-Soaked Peaches and macadamia nuts. I am definitely one for indulging, but it has to be worth it and completely delicious. Otherwise, what's the point?

TISANE DU BERGER DU PÂTISSIER DU CHÂTEAU | TEA INFUSION FROM LE PÂTISSIER DU CHÂTEAU

MAKES ABOUT 3½ OZ (100 G)

1¾ oz (50 g) fresh lemon verbena
1¾ oz (50 g) fresh mint
1¾ oz (50 g) fresh chamomile flowers
½ tsp orange blossom water

Le Pâtissier du Château is a perfect little tearoom a short walk away from the Grimaud castle, and if there's ever a cloudy day, it's a great place to have a chocolat chaud or one of their unique tea infusions. Chamomile and lemon verbena grow in the wild everywhere in France and Britain, so see if you can get your hands on any. This combination is also excellent if you don't have time to dry them: just put a few leaves of each fresh herb straight into hot water. If, like me, you have fennel growing nearby, you can dry and infuse the leaves in the same way.

Tie the herbs in 3 bunches and hang them upside down in a dry place for two weeks, or until dried out completely. Carefully pick off the dried chamomile flowers and the lemon verbena and mint leaves, and put them in a clean, dry, airtight plastic container. Drizzle the orange blossom water over them and keep the box sealed until use.

To make the infusion, pour fresh boiling water over 1–2 tablespoons per cup (it helps to have a teapot with a filter, otherwise you'll need a tea strainer). Infuse for 3 minutes before pouring into cups. Serve with the Mango-Almond Cookies (opposite).

BISCUITS À LA MANGUE ET AUX AMANDES | MANGO-ALMOND COOKIES

MAKES 20

2 oz (60 g) dried mango
6½ tbsp (1¾ oz/50 g)
ground almonds
⅓ cup (1¾ oz/50 g) whole almonds
¾ cup plus 2½ tbsp (6½ oz/200 g)
unrefined superfine sugar
3½ tbsp (1¾ oz/50 g) egg whites
(about 2 free-range large eggs)
unrefined confectioners' sugar,
for dusting

These started life as a mistake but turned out to be a pretty tasty one, so they've snuck into the book. They're a bit like a cross between the classic Provençal cookie calissons d'Aix and Italian amaretti cookies. They were born to accompany un café au lait.

Line a sheet pan with parchment paper. Put the mango and both types of almonds into a blender or food processor and blitz. Process until the nuts and fruit have broken down to a fine consistency and molded together; this will take about 5 minutes. Have the sugar and egg whites in two separate containers at the ready. Still blitzing, pour in 2 tablespoons sugar and then a little of the egg white. Keep adding a little of each until the mixture turns into a thick and chunky paste. Scrape it into a bowl and set aside, covered with plastic wrap, to rest for 10 minutes.

Use 2 teaspoons to make almond shapes (known as *quenelles*) with the paste: spoon out a little of the mixture with one teaspoon, and use the other spoon to scoop and push it off the first spoon to create an egg shape. Continue moving it from one spoon to the other until you are happy with the shape, then gently drop it onto the lined sheet pan. Make the rest of the cookies, then dust them generously with confectioners' sugar. Leave to rest at room temperature for 3 hours or up to overnight.

Preheat the oven to 325°F (170°C). Bake the cookies for 25–30 minutes, rotating the pan 180 degrees halfway through baking, until all are evenly golden brown with a crisp layer on top. Remove and leave to cool. Use a slotted spatula to gently lift them off the parchment paper. Store in a dry, airtight container for up to 4 months.

GUIMAUVES À LA VANILLE ET FLEUR D'ORANGER | VANILLA AND ORANGE BLOSSOM MARSHMALLOWS

MAKES ABOUT 24

13 gelatin sheets (leaves),
⅔–¾ oz (20–25 g)
2 cups (14½ oz/450 g) unrefined
superfine sugar
1 cup (8 fl oz/250 ml) water
2 free-range large egg whites
2 tsp natural beet coloring
1 tbsp vanilla extract
1 tsp orange blossom water
3–4 tbsp cornstarch
1 tbsp unrefined
confectioners' sugar

Who could resist these pillowy homemade marshmallows? I happened to spot them one Easter in an old-fashioned glass jar in the window of La Pause Douceur, a fabulous chocolaterie in St. Tropez. I finally learned how to make them years later at the Ledbury restaurant in Notting Hill and adapted them to make vanilla and orange blossom flavor. These marshmallows have been a particular hit at kids' parties and are pictured here with my Sénéquier Nougat (page 100). You could also try flavoring them with lemon or peppermint extract.

Start by softening the gelatin sheets in a bowl of cold water for 5 minutes. Heat the sugar and water until dissolved. Squeeze out any excess water from the gelatin and gradually whisk it into the sugar syrup. Increase the heat and, using a thermometer, cook until the mixture reaches 252°F (122°C). Meanwhile, begin whisking the egg whites in a stand mixer until stiff peaks form. Continue beating while slowly trickling in the hot syrup, a little at a time, until everything is mixed in; this takes about 7 minutes. Beat in the beet coloring, vanilla extract and orange blossom water and whisk for another 10 minutes until the bowl is cool. The marshmallow mixture should be thick and glossy.

In a small bowl, mix the cornstarch and confectioners' sugar and lightly sprinkle a layer onto a baking pan lined with parchment paper. Pour the marshmallow mixture onto the pan and spread it out with a spatula to 1¼ inches (3 cm) high. Leave it to firm up for about 1 hour. Dust another pan generously with the cornstarch mixture. Use a sharp knife to cut the marshmallow into ¾-inch (2-cm) squares and transfer them to the second pan. Dust the cubes with the cornstarch mixture, making sure all the sides are lightly coated. Eat them right away or store in a dry airtight container for up to one week, and coat them with an extra dusting of the cornstarch mixture to freshen them up.

NOUGAT SÉNÉQUIER | SÉNÉQUIER NOUGAT

MAKES ABOUT 1¼ LB (600 G)

1 cup (5 oz/150 g) whole almonds
¾ cup (3½ oz/100 g) pistachios
2 tbsp plus 2 tsp (1¼ fl oz/40 ml)
free-range egg whites
¾ cup plus 1 tbsp (5¾ oz/165 g)
unrefined superfine sugar
1 cup plus 1 tbsp (8½ fl oz/265 ml)
orange blossom honey
4 sheets edible rice paper
or wafer paper

One of the things I most looked forward to when I worked at the Sénéquier bakery was seeing how they make their famous nougat. It's created in a special room with a gigantic metal cauldron that mixes the honey caramel, ready for pouring into the egg whites. Nougat is a fantastic gift and is easy to make with a stand mixer and a thermometer; the key is getting the caramel temperature high enough so that it sets. This recipe makes a firm but wonderfully chewy nougat.

Preheat the oven to 400°F (200°C). Spread the nuts on a sheet pan and toast for 7–8 minutes, until lightly toasted. Put them in a bowl and set aside. Prepare a mug of hot water and place two wooden spoons in it. Line a baking pan with parchment paper and lay out two sheets of rice paper next to each other on the pan and overlapping a little to make a letter-size sheet. Pour the egg whites into a mixing bowl. Everything needs to be ready before you start the caramel, because once you mix the nuts into the nougat, you have to act fast before it sets.

Put the sugar and honey in a saucepan and place over medium heat. (I always hold the honey pot under the hot water tap for a few minutes first so that it pours more easily.) Swirl the pan from side to side to make sure all the sugar dissolves into the honey. Check the temperature with a thermometer and simmer until the sugar reaches 175°F (80°C). At this point, increase the heat and start whisking the egg whites at medium speed to form stiff peaks. Once the caramel reaches 265°F (130°C) and the egg whites are ready, very carefully and slowly drip about 1 tablespoon caramel into the egg whites. Return the pan to the heat and continue to beat, to start the cooking process and prevent the whites from splitting. Bring the caramel to just before it reaches 325°F (170°C), keeping a close eye on the temperature, then remove from the heat and slowly trickle it into the egg whites, beating continuously. Take care not to drip any hot caramel onto the bowl or whisk, or your hands. Aim it straight into the whites, and keep whisking at high speed until all the caramel is mixed in. Keep mixing until the bowl starts to feel cool and the nougat texture becomes rougher. This will take 8–10 minutes. At this point, reduce the speed, add the nuts and make sure they all are coated in the mixture. Use the hot wooden spoons to scrape the mixture onto the rice paper. Flatten out the nougat with one spoon, dipping it back into the hot water occasionally, and use the other spoon to help push it down. Place two more sheets of rice paper over the top. Push down on the paper with clean, dry hands and leave to cool for about 3 hours. After the nougat has set, use a knife that has been run under hot water and then dried to cut it into the desired shapes. Eat immediately, or store for up to 3 weeks, wrapped in plastic wrap or parchment paper (making sure the wrap touches all the edges), in an airtight container. It needs to be covered properly to avoid it absorbing too much moisture.

SCONES AU BABEURRE AVEC CONFITURE DE FRAMBOISES ET CRÈME D'EAU DE ROSE | BUTTERMILK SCONES WITH RASPBERRY JAM AND ROSEWATER CREAM

MAKES 10

2¾ cups (14 oz/440 g) all-purpose flour, plus extra for dusting
2 tsp baking powder
½ cup plus 3 tbsp (4½ oz/140 g) unrefined superfine sugar
7 tbsp (3½ oz/100 g) cold unsalted butter, diced, plus extra for greasing
2 tsp vanilla extract
1 cup plus 2 tbsp (9 fl oz/280 ml) buttermilk
raspberry jam, to serve

FOR THE ROSEWATER CREAM
5 tsp unrefined superfine sugar
1 free-range large egg yolk
1 cup (8 oz/250 g) mascarpone
1 tsp rose water

There used to be a stunning but hard-to-find rose farm just off the Pampelonne. I'd driven past it hundreds of times before I knew it existed. These scones take me back to when I first opened the rickety gate and was greeted by a hazy puff of rose perfume. But beware, the scent is strong and one drop too many can end in une catastrophe.

Sift the flour and baking powder into a bowl and add the sugar. Rub the butter in with your fingertips until it forms fine crumbs, then stir in the vanilla and buttermilk. Bring the dough together and work it lightly with your hands to bring it into a ball. Wrap it in plastic wrap and chill in the fridge for 1 hour.

Meanwhile, prepare the rosewater cream. Whisk the sugar and egg yolk with a handheld electric mixer for about 5 minutes, until it's pale and the sugar has dissolved. Add the mascarpone and rose water and continue to mix until just combined. Set aside, in the fridge if making it in advance.

Preheat the oven to 400°F (200°C). Lightly grease a sheet pan and line it with parchment paper. Remove the dough from the fridge. Working it as little as possible, roll the dough out on a lightly floured surface to about 1¾–2 inches (4.5–5 cm) thick. Cut out scones with a 2¾-inch (7-cm) biscuit cutter, or use a glass. Place on the prepared sheet pan and bake for 10–15 minutes, or until the bottoms are golden. Leave them to cool on a wire rack for at least 10 minutes before eating. Serve with the rose water cream and plenty of raspberry jam.

LA TARTE AUX ABRICOTS DE LA MAMAN | LA MAMAN'S APRICOT TART

SERVES 6

¾ cup plus 1½ tbsp (4¼ oz/135 g) all-purpose flour
¼ cup (1 oz/30 g) ground almonds
½ cup (1¾ oz/50 g) unrefined confectioners' sugar
finely grated zest of ½ unwaxed lemon
6 tbsp (2¾ oz/85 g) cold unsalted butter, diced, plus extra for greasing
1 free-range large egg yolk
1 tbsp cold water
11 oz (350 g) fresh apricots, halved and pitted
1 tbsp unrefined superfine sugar
scant ½ cup (4½ oz/140 g) apricot jam
sea salt
Honey-Lavender Ice Cream (page 242) or crème fraîche, to serve

La Maman is my mum, Lydia, and this is her apricot tart. Whenever she is invited for dinner at someone's house she whips up one of these heavenly tarts without fail as a thank-you gift. It's a simple recipe, but when served with the silky-smooth Honey-Lavender Ice Cream on page 242, it tastes anything but.

First, make the pastry. Put the flour, ground almonds, confectioners' sugar, lemon zest and a pinch of salt in a stand mixer and beat at slow speed. Add the diced butter and beat for 4 minutes, then add the egg yolk and cold water and beat faster for 5 more minutes. The dough will begin to come together into a ball. Remove and wrap the dough in plastic wrap. Chill in the fridge for at least 1 hour.

Preheat the oven to 325°F (170°C) and grease an 8-inch (20-cm) tart pan with a removable bottom. Grate a thin layer of the chilled pastry to cover the bottom of the pan. Use your fingers to press the pastry into a nice thin layer and grate some more for the edges. Make sure there are no gaps and the pan is neatly lined all over with pastry. This needs to be done swiftly so the pastry doesn't get too warm. If it seems overworked, place the pan in the fridge for 15 minutes to cool. Prick the bottom of the pastry lightly with a fork and bake on the top shelf of the oven for 20 minutes, or until very lightly colored.

Meanwhile, arrange the apricots cut side up, on a sheet pan lined with parchment paper, sprinkle with the superfine sugar and bake in the oven on the shelf below the pastry for about 30–40 minutes, or until roasted and soft. Remove and let the pastry and apricots cool completely. Carefully remove the pastry from the pan and place it on a serving plate. Spoon the apricot jam into the pastry to cover the base and arrange the apricot halves on top, leaving behind any juices that have seeped out. Serve with the ice cream or a spoonful of crème fraîche.

LA TARTE TROPÉZIENNE | ST. TROPEZ TART

SERVES 10

FOR THE BRIOCHE
5 tsp whole milk
2 tsp fresh yeast,
or 1¼ tsp instant yeast
1¼ cups (7 oz/200 g) bread flour
2 free-range large eggs plus
2 yolks, lightly beaten
2 tbsp unrefined superfine sugar
2 tsp orange blossom water
½ cup (4 oz/125 g) soft
unsalted butter
sea salt

FOR THE FILLING
1 vanilla bean
1 cup plus 1 tbsp (9 fl oz/270 ml)
whole milk
½ cup (4 oz/120 g) yolks
(6-7 free-range large eggs)
½ cup (3½ oz/100 g) unrefined
superfine sugar, plus 1½ tbsp
6 tbsp (1½ oz/45 g) cornstarch
6½ tbsp (3½ fl oz/100 ml)
heavy cream
1 tsp vanilla extract
1½ tsp almond extract
unrefined confectioners' sugar,
for dusting
2½ tbsp pistachios, chopped

This cake was named in 1956 in honor of Brigitte Bardot while she was filming in town. Today, it's the cake of St. Tropez and is sold all over the region. This recipe is modeled on the secret one at the Sénéquier bakery. It's a delightfully sweet brioche-tart with a delicate almond crème pâtissière.

First, make the brioche dough. Heat the milk until lukewarm and add the yeast and 1 heaped teaspoon of the flour. Set aside for 30 minutes, covered with plastic wrap.

In the bowl of a stand mixer, beat three-quarters of the eggs, the sugar and a pinch of salt together. Add the yeast mixture, and spoon in the rest of the flour and orange blossom water. Mix until everything is just combined, then cover with a tea towel and leave to rest for 30 minutes. Now, set the mixer to a slow speed and begin spooning in the soft butter, letting each addition combine with the dough before adding the next. Once everything is incorporated, increase the speed and mix until the dough looks elastic and shiny. Scrape into a clean, dry bowl, cover with plastic wrap and leave to prove in the fridge overnight.

Line a sheet pan with parchment paper, tip the chilled dough onto it and shape into a flat circle, roughly 1¼-1½ inches (3-4 cm) high. Cover lightly with plastic wrap and leave to rise for 2-3 hours in a warm, dry place, until doubled in size. Preheat the oven to 400°F (200°C). Once the dough has risen, brush the remaining egg all over it with a pastry brush. Bake for about 25-30 minutes, until the top is gorgeous and golden. Remove and leave to cool completely on a wire rack.

Prepare the pastry cream at least a good few hours before the brioche is ready, as it needs time to cool. Split the vanilla pod in half lengthwise and scrape out the seeds with the back of a knife. Put the vanilla seeds and pod in a large saucepan along with the milk and heat gently for 10 minutes. In a large bowl, whisk together the egg yolks and the ½ cup (3½ oz/100 g) superfine sugar until pale, then stir in the

cornstarch. Slowly add the vanilla-infused milk to the eggs a little at a time, mixing constantly to prevent the eggs from curdling. Carefully return the mixture to the saucepan and gently bring it to a boil, stirring frequently, for 5–10 minutes, until it thickens. Remove from the heat, pour the mixture through a sieve placed over a bowl and stir it through to remove any lumps, discarding the vanilla pod. Cover with plastic wrap touching the surface to prevent a skin from forming, leave to cool and then chill.

Once cool, whip the cream with the 1½ tablespoons superfine sugar and the vanilla and almond extracts until light and fluffy. Loosen the cooled pastry cream with a whisk. Gently fold the whipped almond cream into the vanilla pastry cream. Slice the cooled brioche in half horizontally and fill with the pastry cream. Top the tart with a dusting of confectioners' sugar and, for an injection of color, some chopped pistachios.

TARTELETTES AUX FRAMBOISES ET FRUITS DE LA PASSION | RASPBERRY AND PASSION FRUIT TARTLETS

MAKES 12

1²⁄₃ cups (6½ oz/200 g) fresh raspberries
2 passion fruits, halved
confectioners' sugar, for dusting

FOR THE SWEET PASTRY
3 cups (15 oz/480 g) all-purpose flour
1 cup plus 3 tbsp (5 oz/150 g) unrefined confectioners' sugar
1½ tsp poppy seeds
finely grated zest of 1 unwaxed lemon
1 cup (7½ oz/225 g) cold unsalted butter, diced, plus extra for greasing
2 free-range large egg yolks
3-4 tbsp cold water
sea salt

FOR THE MASCARPONE CREAM
1 free-range large egg yolk
2 tbsp unrefined superfine sugar
1 cup (8 oz/250 g) mascarpone
1 tsp orange blossom water

These are one of my signature tarts. They're particularly memorable for me because I took them to my first meeting with my publisher, so to me they're known as BD (book deal) tartlets! The pastry shells and cream can be prepared the day before, but they should be assembled à la minute to keep them as fresh as possible.

Make the pastry by combining the first four ingredients and a pinch of salt in the bowl of a stand mixer. Slowly add the butter and beat at medium speed for 5 minutes, then add the egg yolks. Add 1 tablespoon cold water and mix for a few minutes (you may need to add more water if the mixture looks dry). Increase the speed and beat until everything comes together into a ball. Wrap in plastic wrap and chill in the fridge for at least 1 hour.

For the cream, put the egg yolk and sugar in a clean mixer bowl. Beat at medium-high speed until they have combined to make a creamy liquid and most of the sugar has dissolved. Add the mascarpone and orange blossom water and whisk for a moment, to bring everything together. Store in the fridge until needed (it keeps for up to 3 days).

Lightly grease twelve 4-inch (10-cm) tartlet pans with removable bottoms. Grate a thin layer of chilled pastry into one of the pans. Use your fingers to press and mold the pastry into the pan. Chill in the fridge, then continue with the rest of the pan. Rest them in the fridge for 15 minutes and preheat the oven to 325°F (170°C). Bake for about 15-20 minutes, until lightly colored but not golden. Leave to cool for a few minutes, then carefully remove the pastry from the pans and cool completely on a wire rack. Spoon some mascarpone cream into each pastry shell and top with a few raspberries. Scoop the passion fruit pulp out and place on top of the raspberries. Lightly dust with confectioners' sugar and serve.

TARTE AU CHOCOLAT BLANC ET AUX PÊCHES À L'AMARETTO | WHITE CHOCOLATE TART WITH AMARETTO-SOAKED PEACHES

SERVES 4

1 cup (5 oz/160 g) all-purpose flour
6½ tbsp (1¾ oz/50 g) unrefined
confectioners' sugar
finely grated zest of 1 small
unwaxed lemon
6 tbsp (3 oz/85 g) cold
unsalted butter, diced,
plus extra for greasing
1 free-range large egg yolk
1 tbsp cold water (if needed)
⅓ cup (1¾ oz/50 g)
macadamia nuts
sea salt

FOR THE PEACHES
5 sweet, firm peaches, pitted and
cut into chunky slices
1 vanilla bean
2 tbsp unrefined superfine sugar
2 tbsp Amaretto

FOR THE WHITE CHOCOLATE GANACHE
4 oz (120 g) white chocolate, finely
chopped
1 tbsp soft unsalted butter
¼ cup (2 fl oz/60 ml) heavy cream

I spent a long time creating something that would do justice to a beautiful bowl of peaches, and I decided that all white was the direction to go: sweet peaches sitting on a lavish blanket of creamy white chocolate and a generous tumble of light, crunchy, buttery nuts. My tasting team, the Parkers, polished this tart off in seconds.

First, make the pastry. Put the first three ingredients and a pinch of salt into the stand mixer and beat at slow speed. Increase the speed, add the diced butter and bring together to form a light crumb consistency. Now add the egg yolk; the pastry should come together into a ball. If the dough is a little dry, add the cold water. Wrap the dough tightly in plastic wrap and chill in the fridge for 2 hours.

Put the peach slices in a saucepan over medium-low heat. Split the vanilla bean in half lengthwise and scrape out the seeds with the back of a knife. Add the sugar, Amaretto and vanilla seeds and pod to the peaches. Simmer for 8–10 minutes, or until the peaches are soft, then leave to cool.

Preheat the oven to 325°F (170°C) and grease an 8-inch (20-cm) tart pan with a removable bottom. Grate the chilled pastry over the pan until the base is covered with a thin layer. Use your fingers to press and flatten the pastry into the pan. Grate over more pastry for the edges, making sure there are no gaps, and finally prick the base with a fork. Do not overwork or let the pastry get too warm; if this occurs, simply chill it in the fridge for another 20 minutes. Bake for 25 minutes, until the top is very slightly colored, then leave to cool completely. Carefully remove it from the pan and place on a serving plate. Increase the oven temperature to 400°F (200°C) and roast the macadamia nuts lightly for about 5 minutes, until toasted and lightly golden. Tip onto a plate.

For the ganache, put the white chocolate and butter in a
heatproof bowl and heat the cream in a small saucepan until
just simmering. Quickly pour it over the chocolate and slowly
mix them together until completely melted and combined.
Scrape into the cooled pastry base and leave to harden for
about 1 hour in the fridge. Leave the peach segments looking
rustic and arrange them on top of the tart. Any leftover juices
are precious: just reduce them in a saucepan over low heat
for 2–3 minutes to create a syrup. Drizzle it over the peaches
and scatter the toasted macadamia nuts on top.

GÂTEAU DE MARIAGE AU CITRON ET AU SAFRAN | LEMON SAFFRON WEDDING CAKE

SERVES 8

good pinch of saffron threads
½ cup (4 oz/120 g) soft
unsalted butter, diced,
plus extra for greasing
¾ cup plus 2½ tbsp (6 oz/180 g)
unrefined superfine sugar
1½ cups (6 oz/180 g) ground
almonds
¾ cup (4 oz/130 g)
all-purpose flour
2 tsp poppy seeds
finely grated zest and juice of
2 unwaxed lemons
4 free-range large eggs,
lightly beaten
1 tsp baking powder

FOR THE ICING
7 tbsp (3½ tbsp/100 g) soft
unsalted butter
⅔ cup (2¾ oz/80 g) unrefined
confectioners' sugar
10 oz (300 g) cream cheese
(at room temperature)
finely grated zest and juice of
1 unwaxed lemon

This is a very special cake. I made it for a girl named Sophie who wanted a lemon drizzle cake included as one of the layers in her wedding cake. I assembled a three-tiered version of this cake on a stage, under spotlights, with hundreds of passersby watching my every icing move.

Preheat the oven to 325°F (170°C), and grease and line two 7-inch (17-cm) cake pans with parchment paper. In a small bowl, add 3 tablespoons hot water and the saffron. Leave to infuse for 10 minutes.

Meanwhile, in the stand mixer, cream the butter and ½ cup plus 1 tbsp (4 oz/120 g) of the sugar until light and fluffy, about 5 minutes. Mix the ground almonds, flour, poppy seeds and lemon zest in a separate bowl. Still beating, slowly trickle a little of the eggs into the creamed butter. Add a tablespoon of the flour mixture and continue alternating between the two until everything is combined. Gently fold in the saffron water, then divide the batter equally between the pans. Bake for 35 minutes, until the top is golden and a skewer inserted comes out clean. While the cake is baking, heat the remaining sugar and the lemon juice in a pan over medium-low heat until dissolved. Increase the heat to let the liquid bubble and form a syrup.

Turn out one of the cakes onto a wire rack, bottom side up, and gently prick it with a toothpick. Spoon the hot syrup over the cake to soak into the sponge, and turn out the second cake to cool on the rack.

For the icing, in the cleaned mixer bowl, cream the butter and confectioners' sugar together until pale and fluffy. In another bowl, whip the cream cheese until fluffy, then drizzle in the lemon juice and fold into the creamed butter. Spread half the icing on top of one of the cakes. Lay the second cake on top and spread the top with the icing. Dust with the lemon zest.

LE GÂTEAU D'ANNIVERSAIRE | THE BIRTHDAY CAKE

SERVES 12

1 cup plus 3 tbsp (10 oz/300 g) soft unsalted butter, diced
1⅓ cups (10 oz/300 g) unrefined superfine sugar
⅔ cup (4½ oz/140 g) firmly packed brown sugar
1 cup (3½ oz/100 g) unsweetened cocoa powder
⅔ cup (5 fl oz/160 ml) buttermilk or sour cream
1 tsp vanilla extract
¼ cup (2 fl oz/60 ml) cold water
1¼ cups (6½ oz/200 g) all-purpose flour
¾ cup (3½ oz/100 g) ground almonds
1 tsp baking powder
1 tsp baking soda
3 free-range large eggs, lightly beaten
1 tbsp Grand Marnier
1 tsp instant coffee granules
sea salt

FOR THE ICING
13 oz (400 g) dark chocolate (at least 70% cacao solids)
1¼ cups (10 fl oz/300 ml) heavy cream
2 tbsp Grand Marnier
1 cup (8 oz/250 g) soft unsalted butter
1½ cups (6 oz/180 g) unrefined confectioners' sugar

This is the ultimate birthday or celebration cake. It's a simple chocolate sponge cake frosted with a sophisticated Grand Marnier icing.

Preheat the oven to 350°F (180°C). Grease two 12-inch (30-cm) springform cake pans and line them with parchment paper. Using a stand mixer or a hand-held electric mixer, cream the butter and both sugars until light and fluffy, about 5 minutes on a fast speed. Combine the cocoa powder, buttermilk, vanilla extract and cold water to make a paste. Sift the dry ingredients except the ground almonds into another bowl with a pinch of salt, then stir in the ground almonds. Now everything comes together: reduce the speed of the mixer, trickle in a little beaten egg and then increase the speed until it combines. Add the rest of the egg a little at a time, taking care not to curdle the mixture. If this occurs, mix in a spoonful of the dry ingredients. Finish adding all the eggs until the batter is lovely and light. Now turn the mixer to a constant medium-slow speed, spoon in some of the cocoa paste, wait for it to be incorporated, then add a spoonful of the flour mixture. Continue adding and alternating the two mixes until everything is combined. Stir in the Grand Marnier. Divide the batter equally between the two pans and bake for 45 minutes to 1 hour, or until a skewer inserted comes out almost clean. Remove and leave to cool to room temperature on a wire rack.

Meanwhile, make the icing. Melt the chocolate in a heatproof bowl set over a pan of simmering water, making sure the bowl does not touch the water. Remove from the heat and very gradually whisk in the cream until it becomes a glossy ganache. Stir in the Grand Marnier and leave to cool to a spreadable consistency. Beat the butter and confectioners' sugar until light and fluffy, then fold it into the chocolate ganache a spoonful at a time. Cover the surface of one of the cakes with icing. Place the other cake on top and fill in the gaps with icing and cover all over. Try not to work the icing too much, as it will lose its shine.

GÂTEAU AUX POIRES CARAMÉLISÉES ET ÉPICES | CARAMELIZED PEAR SPICE CAKE

SERVES 4

FOR THE PEARS
3½ tbsp (1¼ oz/50 g) unsalted butter
2 tbsp unrefined superfine sugar
1 vanilla bean
3 ripe but firm pears, cored and quartered
1 tsp ground cardamom
2 whole cloves

FOR THE CAKE
⅔ cup (5 oz/150 g) soft unsalted butter, plus extra for greasing
½ cup plus 1 tbsp (4 oz/125 g) unrefined superfine sugar
⅔ cup (2¾ oz/80 g) ground almonds
7 tbsp (2¼ oz/70 g) all-purpose flour
1 tsp baking powder
½ tsp ground cinnamon
pinch of freshly grated nutmeg
finely grated zest of 1 unwaxed lemon
2 free-range large eggs, lightly beaten
crème fraîche, to serve

This was inspired by a pear torte at L'Anima restaurant in London, and it has since become a classic of mine. When I worked there, I did tend to "dis-pear" into the pastry kitchen when pears were in season. Pear chocolate tart, filo-wrapped pears baked in spices, pear sorbet, pear and nut pastries . . . nuff said!

Heat the butter and sugar in a saucepan over high heat until golden and sticky. Split the vanilla bean lengthwise and scrape out the seeds with the back of a knife. Add the seeds and pod to the pan, along with the pears. Reduce the heat to a simmer and cook for 3 minutes, turning the pears occasionally, then remove from the heat and leave to cool.

Preheat the oven to 325°F (170°C) and grease and line an 8-inch (20-cm) springform cake pan with parchment paper. Cream the butter and sugar in a mixing bowl until pale and fluffy. In a separate bowl, mix together the dry ingredients and lemon zest. Increase the speed and slowly drizzle in a little of the beaten eggs, followed by a spoonful of the dry ingredients. Continue adding alternately until everything is incorporated. Pour the batter into the prepared pan and smooth with a spatula to create an even top. Slice the cooled pears lengthwise into slices ⅜ inch (1 cm) thick. Arrange the pears in a pattern on top of the batter and bake for about 1–1½ hours, until the top is cooked through and a skewer inserted comes out almost clean. Any leftover cooking juices from the pears can be simmered for 10–15 minutes, or until reduced to a syrup, then poured over the baked cake. Cool to room temperature before serving with a good dollop of crème fraîche.

DRINKS AND CANAPÉS
APÉRITIF ET CANAPÉS

THE FAMOUS St. Tropez light is at its best when the sun starts setting over the bay and the boats are bringing up their anchors for the journey back home. Many artists, such as Matisse and Signac, have captured the way the light falls delicately across the town and the beautiful surroundings, and even today St. Tropez is still just a fishing village filled with artists displaying their work. After an evening stroll around the galleries and the painters lining the port, the next stop is an ice-cold apéritif in one of the cafés, perhaps a *citron pressé* at Le Café Clemenceau, which is perfect for spying on the *boules* players in the Place des Lices. My Apéritif de Pampelonne, made with ruby-red blood orange granita, is inspired by the delicious cocktails on offer at the beach bars—a drink for watching the sun go down as the light gently fades and the water in the bay becomes dark and velvety.

Inland, in addition to the constant summer concert from the crickets, there are rows upon rows of beautiful vineyards offering their own versions of rosé, the perfect summer wine. Château de Pampelonne, Château Minty and Domaine de Bertaud Belieu have all created slightly different varieties. A glass of Rosé Sur La Mer or Cassis Champagne à La Giscle sipped on the balcony is the perfect preparation for the night's festivities.

August 15 is a national holiday in France, and parties are held to celebrate all over the region. During the evening, St. Tropez buzzes with cocktail revelries in private gardens and secret roof-top soirées. In Port Grimaud we hold an *anchoïade* party on our street—everybody brings a bottle of rosé, we listen to the Gipsy Kings and feast away on canapés. Other delicious *amuse-bouches* might include classic Eggplant Caviar, Risotto Balls with Leek, Thyme and Fennel Seeds and rich Chicken Liver Pâté from La Môle. It's simple to make a few tempting nibbles that will disappear in seconds. The trick is to remember that drinks and canapés are just the beginning of what's to come!

APÉRITIF MANUKA DU MIGON | THE MIGON'S MANUKA COCKTAIL

SERVES 2

1²⁄₃ cups (14 fl oz/400 ml) freshly
squeezed orange juice
(about 6 oranges)
4 tsp Manuka honey
5 tbsp (2½ fl oz/75 ml) vodka
2 tsp Monin sugar syrup
2 generous sprigs fresh sage
few ice cubes

Le Migon, the last beach restaurant on the Pampelonne stretch, serves beautiful seafood dishes surrounded by rustic driftwood furniture and old-fashioned nautical treasures. Even the battered sign is painted on an old fishing boat. The cocktails are simple with modern touches; this one uses Manuka honey, which is thought to have healing properties.

Pour the orange juice, honey, vodka, syrup and a few ice cubes into a cocktail shaker or large jar with a lid and shake well. Put a few ice cubes into two tumblers and divide the cocktail between them. Finish with a sprig of sage in each glass. The idea is that you smell the sage leaves while you are drinking, which adds another dimension to the drink.

APÉRITIF DE PAMPELONNE | PAMPELONNE COCKTAIL

SERVES 2

FOR THE GRANITA
2 cups (16 fl oz/500 ml) freshly
squeezed blood orange juice
(about 7 oranges)
finely grated zest of 3 oranges
½ cup plus 1 tbsp (4¼ oz/about
130 g) unrefined superfine sugar

FOR THE COCKTAILS
½ cup (4 fl oz/120 ml)
Dubonnet Rouge
2½ tbsp tonic water

Sometimes you need a small pick-me-up to get you in the mood for the evening, and I stumbled upon this drink in one of the beach bars along the Pampelonne. It's traditionally made with fresh orange juice, but I like it with my blood orange granita, as it looks great for a party. Granita is delicious as a dessert too, especially when served in a martini glass with a dollop of vanilla ice cream.

Mix all the granita ingredients together in a freezerproof container until the sugar has completely dissolved. You might need a little more or less sugar, depending on how sweet the oranges are. Place the container in the freezer until the liquid has frozen. Remove it and let it thaw for about 15 minutes, then start to scrape away at the ice with a fork, in forward strokes. After a few minutes you should have a bright red mound of icy crystals. Half fill two tumbler glasses with the blood orange granita. Mix the Dubonnet and tonic water together and pour on top of the granita. *Bon apéritif!*

CASSIS CHAMPAGNE À LA GISCLE

CASSIS CHAMPAGNE À LA GISCLE

SERVES 2

3½ tbsp (1¾ fl oz/50 ml) cassis liqueur
about ¾ cup (6½ fl oz/200 ml) champagne or sparkling wine, well chilled
2 fresh raspberries

This is a simple drink, but wherever I am in the world it takes me to my pontoon overlooking Port Grimaud's canal, otherwise known as La Giscle. This is a great drink for before a night out, and the combination of cassis with champagne or sparkling wine is a tough one to beat!

Add half of the cassis to each champagne flute. Slowly pour half of the champagne or sparkling wine into each glass and pop a raspberry on top. *Et voilà!*

ROSÉ EN MER

ROSÉ ON THE SEA

SERVES 2

1¼ cups (10 fl oz/300 ml) rosé wine, well chilled
1 tsp orange blossom water
2 tsp Monin sugar syrup
2 tsp unrefined superfine sugar
pared zest of ½ unwaxed lemon and a few drops juice
few ice cubes

Rosé is the drink of the south coast, and vineyards such as Château de Pampelonne and Château Minty produce some wonderful pastel-pink varieties. I've taken this apéritif everywhere and even made it on a small dinghy for a picnic—a balancing act to say the least!

Make sure the rosé has been chilling in the fridge for a few hours. Pour everything except the lemon zest into a pitcher and stir with some ice cubes. Pour into large wineglasses and garnish with a strip of lemon zest.

CITRON PRESSÉ DU CAFÉ CLEMENCEAU | CAFÉ CLEMENCEAU'S CITRON PRESSÉ

SERVES 2

finely grated zest of 4 unwaxed
lemons, plus juice of 6
few ice cubes
½ cup (4 fl oz/120 ml) cold water
or Badoit mineral water
8-9 tsp unrefined superfine sugar
few sprigs fresh mint

*Right on the corner of the Place des Lices is the popular Café Clemenceau.
It reminds me of a Parisian restaurant, with the tables bundled up close
together so that your elbows bash not-so-politely into your neighbors.
Nobody minds, though, because these are the best seats in the house for
people-watching, with panoramic views of a crowded street leading back to
the port. If I can elbow my way to a table, there's nothing more refreshing
than this citron pressé.*

Put some ice cubes into two tall glasses. Divide the lemon
juice and zest between the glasses, stirring to chill the
juice. Pour in the water and begin adding the sugar to taste,
mixing and tasting until you get the right level. Serve with
fresh mint sprigs.

PANIER DE CRUDITÉS DE PATRICE | PATRICE'S CRUDITÉ BASKET

SERVES 6

4 free-range large eggs
2 large tomatoes
4 carrots
2 Belgian endives
1 cauliflower
1 celery heart
1–2 bunches radishes

FOR THE ANCHOÏADE MAYONNAISE
(makes 1⅔ cups/14 oz/400 g)
1 free-range large egg yolk
1¼ cups (10 fl oz/300 ml) sunflower oil
1 tbsp cider vinegar
juice of ½ lemon
2½ tbsp Anchoïade (page 133)
sea salt and black pepper

Patrice de Colmont is the owner of the successful beach restaurant Club 55, which started when his parents casually prepared food for the crew of the Brigitte Bardot film Et Dieu Créa la Femme (And God Created Woman) *from an old beach shack. After the film sets cleared away, the demand for his mother's simple beach food became greater and greater. Today, at peak season Patrice welcomes 800 to 900 people over two or three sittings. One of their signature dishes is le panier de crudités, an enormous mound of fresh homegrown vegetables from their farm and some hard-boiled eggs, all accompanied by anchoïade mayonnaise for dipping.*

In a medium pan, boil the eggs for 9 minutes, then remove and run under cold water for a moment to cool. Wash the vegetables and arrange in a basket or serving platter.

For the mayonnaise, whisk the egg yolk in a clean, dry mixing bowl and trickle in a little oil, whisking constantly. Continue adding oil very gradually, a little at a time, allowing the oil to thicken and whiten the yolk. After you've added about half the oil, beat in the cider vinegar, then continue slowly trickling in the remaining oil. Add the rest of the ingredients and taste to check the seasoning. Serve the crudités with the mayonnaise and eggs on the side.

ANCHOÏADE | ANCHOVY PASTE

MAKES ¾ CUP
(6½ OZ/200 G)

⅓ cup (1¾ oz/50 g) pitted
black olives
⅓ cup (1¾ oz/50 g) pitted
green olives
2–3 tbsp extra-virgin olive oil
1 tsp capers
½ clove garlic
8 anchovy fillets
1 tbsp cider vinegar
pinch of sugar
4 sun-dried tomatoes, chopped
½ shallot, chopped

This rich, special, caviar-like paste is typically served on toasted bread for an amuse-bouche, but I also like to stir it through pasta as a quick supper. I make it in large quantities and store it in the fridge to use in dressings or with fried fish.

Put everything in a blender and pulse-blend, stopping once or twice to stir and scrape down the sides. Blend to a coarse paste and taste to double-check the seasoning. Done! Store in a sealed container in the fridge for 3 days.

TAPENADE | OLIVE PASTE

MAKES 1¼ CUPS
(9½ OZ/300 G)

⅔ cup (3½ oz/100 g) pitted
black olives
⅓ cup (1¾ oz/50 g) pitted
green olives
2½ tbsp (1¼ oz/40 g) capers
3 anchovy fillets
few shavings lemon zest
2 tbsp extra-virgin olive oil
1 tsp white wine vinegar
2 tsp balsamic vinegar
handful chopped fresh cilantro

This humble olive paste is legendary, whether at picnics on the beach rocks or secret roof-top parties. It's a dark, rustic dip that's amazing served with cooked chicken or fish.

Place everything in a blender and blitz to make a smooth paste. Store in a sealed container in the fridge for up to 4 days.

CAVIAR D'AUBERGINE | EGGPLANT CAVIAR

SERVES 4

2 large eggplants
6 cloves garlic
2 sprigs fresh rosemary
2 tbsp olive oil
1 shallot, finely diced
2 batches Merlot Dressing
(page 59)
sea salt and black pepper

TO SERVE
sourdough bread or
baguette, sliced
3½ tbsp (1¾ oz/50 g)
crème fraîche
handful fresh basil leaves
extra-virgin olive oil

Sometimes known as "poor man's caviar," this is made from the rich, silky pulp of a baked eggplant. It's typically Provençal, although I perfected this recipe at L'Anima restaurant, where it's served with creamy burrata cheese. Spread it on grilled sourdough or baguette slices.

Preheat the oven to 400°F (200°C). Slice the eggplants in half lengthwise and sprinkle a generous pinch of salt over the insides. Leave for 5–10 minutes, then pat dry with paper towels. Using a sharp knife, score the flesh in a crisscross pattern, cutting no more than ¼ inch (5 mm) deep. Quarter the garlic cloves and stick them into the gaps in the eggplants. Snip small sprigs of rosemary and stick them into the flesh, season it with salt and pepper and sprinkle with olive oil. Sandwich the halves back together, wrap them separately in aluminum foil and twist both ends to seal tightly. Bake for 40–45 minutes, until soft when pressed.

Remove and cool for a few minutes before opening up the packages and scooping out the eggplant flesh onto a cutting board, along with the garlic and rosemary leaves. Chop the flesh, gather it into a saucepan and simmer to reduce the juices for about 3 minutes over medium heat. Leave to cool to room temperature and store in the fridge until needed. It's even better when made the day before.

Just before eating, stir in the shallot, half of the fresh basil leaves, torn, and the Merlot dressing. Toast some sourdough, cut it into bite-sized pieces and spoon on some caviar with a small dollop of crème fraîche. Garnish with the rest of the fresh basil leaves and a final drizzle of extra-virgin olive oil.

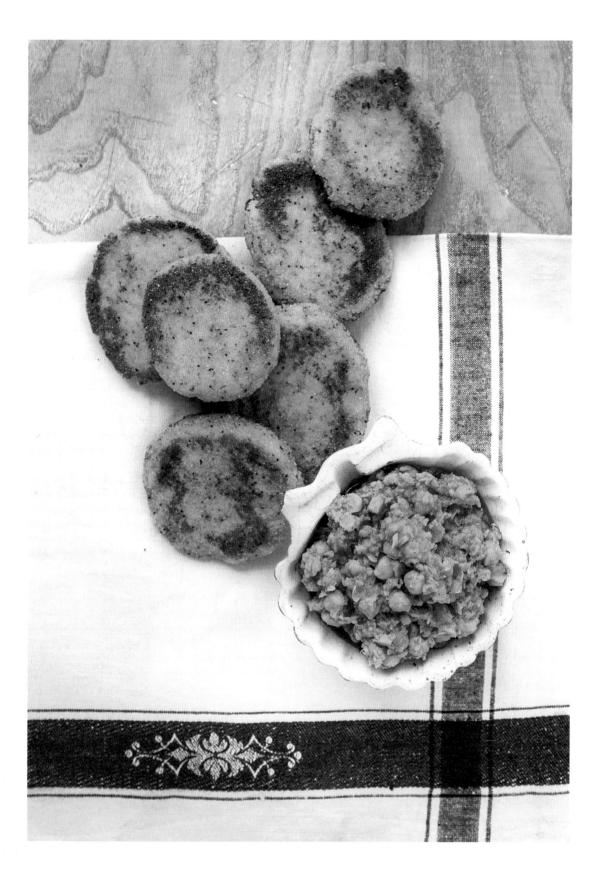

GALETTES DE POLENTA ET YAOURT | POLENTA AND YOGURT GALETTES

MAKES 20 GALETTES

1 cup (7 oz/210 g) quick-cook polenta
¾ cup plus 2 tbsp (7 fl oz/210 ml) Greek yogurt
2 tbsp whole-wheat flour, plus extra for dusting
1 tsp chopped fresh rosemary
1 tsp baking powder
½ tsp poppy seeds
1 tsp sea salt
1 tbsp olive oil
black pepper

When I'm having people over, I make these galettes to dip into La Pesquière's Hummus with Roasted Sweet Potato (below). I must warn you that people tend to gobble them up so quickly that you may need quite an interval before dinner.

Mix all the ingredients except the oil together in a bowl until it forms a soft dough. Wrap in plastic wrap and chill in the fridge for 45 minutes. Remove and divide into 20 balls, then roll each one out to ¼ inch (5 mm) thick on a lightly floured surface. Heat the olive oil in a frying pan over medium-high heat and fry the galettes in batches for about 1–2 minutes on each side, until golden. Serve warm with dips or lightly salted butter.

HUMUS DE LA PESQUIÈRE ET PATATE DOUCE RÔTIE | LA PESQUIÈRE'S HUMMUS WITH ROASTED SWEET POTATO

MAKES ABOUT 2 CUPS (14 OZ/440 G)

5½ oz (160 g) sweet potato, cut into chunks
8 tbsp olive oil
1 clove garlic, diced
1 small shallot, diced
1 tsp ground turmeric
1 tsp paprika
2 tbsp lemon juice
1 cup (6½ oz/200 g) rinsed and drained canned chickpeas
sea salt and black pepper

La Pesquière is one of the oldest restaurants in town and you're always welcomed there with a small bowl of chickpeas seasoned with cumin and chopped raw shallots. Roasted sweet potatoes add extra texture, but make sure you keep the chickpeas mostly whole, in the spirit of La Pesquière.

Preheat the oven to 350°F (180°C). Put the sweet potatoes on a baking pan with a splash of olive oil and season with salt and pepper. Bake for about 40 minutes, or until soft and sticky. Remove and leave to cool for 5 minutes, then place in the blender along with all the ingredients except the chickpeas. Season with salt and pepper and pulse-blend to break everything up into a rough paste. Taste to check the seasoning. Add the chickpeas and pulse-blend briefly to combine, without breaking them all up. Serve with the Polenta and Yogurt Galettes, above.

PÂTÉ DE FOIE DE VOLAILLE DE LA MÔLE | CHICKEN LIVER PÂTÉ FROM LA MÔLE

SERVES 8 AS A CANAPÉ

1²⁄₃ lb (800 g) chicken livers
3 tbsp olive oil
4 tsp unsalted butter
1 onion, diced
handful fresh basil
1 clove garlic, diced
3 tbsp brandy
7 anchovy fillets
freshly grated nutmeg
few drops lemon juice
¾ cup (3½ oz/100 g) toasted
  pistachios, chopped
baguette, sliced, to serve

We joke in my family that when we visit one of our local restaurants, L'Auberge de la Môle, we end up eating so much rich, delicious food that we need a break of two or three years to forget how full we were last time. One of their specialties is pâté, which they serve in traditional earthenware casserole dishes. I make it to serve as a canapé on bite-sized slices of baguette with a sprinkle of chopped pistachios on top.

Bring a pan of salted water to a boil, add the chicken livers and cook for about 5 minutes, until tender and cooked through. Remove and leave to cool. Next, heat 2 tablespoons of the olive oil and the butter in a large pan over medium heat. Add the onion and cook gently, without letting it color. Finely chop the stalks from the basil, then add them to the pan along with the garlic. Add the brandy and bring to a boil, then remove and leave to cool.

Next, put the livers, onion, basil leaves and all the remaining ingredients except the pistachios in a food processor and blitz until lovely and smooth. Check the seasoning and transfer to your preferred container, then into the fridge overnight. I learned from L'Auberge that it's important to apply pressure to the pâté, so I recommend placing something heavy on top. Serve spread on baguette slices, sprinkled with chopped pistachios.

CALAMARS DE CHEZ FUCHS | CHEZ FUCHS'S CALAMARI

SERVES 4 AS A STARTER

2 cups (16 fl oz/500 ml)
sunflower oil
1¼ cups (6½ oz/200 g)
all-purpose flour
2 free-range large eggs
1¾ cups (6½ oz/200 g) dried
sourdough bread crumbs
2 squid, about 13 oz (400 g),
cleaned and sliced into ⅜-inch
(1-cm) rings
2 handfuls fresh flat-leaf parsley
leaves, roughly chopped
2 cloves garlic, finely chopped
1 lemon, cut into wedges
sea salt and black pepper

Chez Fuchs was a locals' hangout serving classic Provençal food right in the center of St. Tropez, a tiny restaurant hidden down one of the city's many cobbled streets above a bar at number 7, rue des Commerçants. On arrival, you were greeted by the chef's plat du jour wafting down the narrow spiral staircase. Sadly Chez Fuchs is now closed, but these calamari are the perfect reminder of the warm sea breeze that used to float in from the balcony. This is also just as delicious served as a main.

Heat the oil in a large, deep saucepan until a pinch of flour sizzles immediately when thrown in. While the oil heats up, put the flour in one bowl; break the eggs into another, beat them lightly and season with salt and pepper. In a separate bowl, mix the bread crumbs with a little salt and pepper. Toss the squid rings in the flour. Dip them a few at a time into the egg, allowing the excess to drip off, then toss in the bread crumbs.

Add half the squid to the hot oil and fry for about 2 minutes, turning and moving them around with tongs to brown all sides evenly. Remove and drain on paper towels. Sprinkle with half the parsley, season with salt and keep warm while you cook the rest. Serve with the garlic, the remaining parsley and plenty of lemon wedges.

SOUPE D'AVOCAT AUX PISTACHES | AVOCADO SOUP WITH PISTACHIOS

SERVES 4 AS A CANAPÉ

2 large ripe avocados
1 cup plus 1 tbsp (8½ fl oz/270 ml)
cold water
juice of ½ lemon
½ clove garlic, finely diced
1 tbsp chopped onion
1 tsp honey
1 tbsp pistachios
2 tbsp extra-virgin olive oil
sea salt and black pepper

When I worked at Gelupo, the ice cream shop in Soho, London, I used to make a creamy avocado sorbet, and it's actually that sweet sorbet that inspired this savory soup. I love to serve it as a canapé in a teacup, or it can be served as an appetizer or starter. The beautiful pea-green color is wonderful—it oozes health in a cup.

Peel and pit the avocados and put them in a blender along with all the other ingredients except the pistachios and olive oil. Season with salt and pepper and blend to make a thick and creamy soup. (Alternatively, put them in a deep container and process with a stick blender.) Taste to check the seasoning and add a little more cold water, depending on how thick you'd like it. Serve at room temperature or chill in the fridge until ready to serve, covered with plastic wrap touching the surface of the liquid to prevent it from going black. It will keep for 1 day in the fridge. When you are ready to serve, roughly chop the pistachios. Serve the soup in teacups with a drizzle of extra-virgin olive oil and a sprinkle of pistachios on top.

BOULETTES DE RISOTTO AU POIREAU, THYM ET GRAINES DE FENOUIL

RISOTTO BALLS WITH LEEK, THYME AND FENNEL SEEDS

SERVES 8

2 tbsp olive oil
2 shallots, diced
½ yellow onion, diced
1 clove garlic, diced
1 tbsp fennel seeds
1½ cups (9½ oz/300 g) Arborio rice
½ cup (4 fl oz/125 ml) white wine
2 cups (16 fl oz/500 ml) hot vegetable stock
1 leek, finely chopped
small bunch fresh thyme
5 oz (150 g) pecorino cheese, grated
1 free-range large egg
1¼ cups (6½ oz/200 g) all-purpose flour
1 lemon, cut into wedges
sea salt and black pepper

These are absolutely winning canapés, the best way to use up any leftover risotto. Whenever I make them they're gobbled up in seconds. You can make the balls in advance and fry them just before eating.

Heat the oil in a saucepan over medium heat. Add the shallots and onion and cook gently until soft and translucent. Add the garlic and fennel seeds and cook for about 2 minutes. Pour in the rice, stirring with a wooden spoon. Make sure the rice is coated in the onions, garlic and fennel seeds, then increase the heat and add the white wine. Stir the rice for 3 minutes, letting it soak up all the alcohol.

Ladle in a few spoonfuls of vegetable stock and stir continuously for 10 minutes, then add the leek and more stock and continue to cook, stirring. Continue adding more stock every few minutes, and after 15–20 minutes the rice should be tender but still with a bit of bite. Sprinkle in the thyme leaves (reserve some for serving) and cheese, season with salt and pepper and add more stock if needed. Leave to cool completely.

Whisk the egg lightly with a fork and season with salt and pepper. Put the flour in a bowl and line a sheet pan with parchment paper. Roll the risotto into golf-ball-sized balls and place on the sheet pan. Dip each one in the egg, letting any excess drip off, then coat them in the flour. Heat 1 tablespoon olive oil in a large saucepan over medium-high heat and fry the risotto balls in batches, turning regularly, until golden and evenly crisp. Serve with a sprinkling of salt, black pepper and more fresh thyme, with lemon wedges to squeeze over them.

BEIGNETS DE BOOKCLUB | BOOK CLUB FRITTERS

SERVES 6

FOR THE DIP
⅔ cup (5 fl oz/150 ml)
Greek yogurt
½ clove garlic, diced
1 tbsp lemon juice
½ tsp honey mustard
2 tbsp extra-virgin olive oil
handful fresh mint, chopped
sea salt and black pepper

FOR THE FRITTERS
1¼ cups (6½ oz/200 g)
all-purpose flour
1⅓ cups (11 fl oz/350 ml) water
4 cups (32 fl oz/1 l) sunflower oil
1 eggplant, sliced ¼ inch
(5 mm) thick
1 cauliflower, cut into
bite-sized chunks
6 large asparagus spears,
cut in half lengthwise
2 zucchini, sliced ¼ inch
(5 mm) thick
1 lemon, cut into wedges

My friends Charli, Felicité, Leo, Roxane and I have a book club, and these fritters made their debut at one of our suppers. The girls insisted on them featuring in the book. In some of the restaurants I've worked in, they're often served with garlic mayonnaise, but here I've gone for a lighter yogurt-based sauce.

Mix all the ingredients for the dip (saving a few mint leaves to garnish) together in a bowl and taste to check the seasoning. Set aside in the fridge.

Put the flour in a bowl and slowly stir in the water to make a batter. Season with salt and pepper. Heat the sunflower oil in a large, deep saucepan over medium-high heat until a pinch of flour sizzles as soon as it's dropped in the pan.

Salt the eggplant slices generously, leave them for a few minutes, then pat dry with paper towels. Toss half the vegetables in the batter, allowing any excess to drip off. Place them carefully in the hot oil to deep-fry in batches, using a long metal spoon to move everything around and turn them over to fry all sides evenly. Fry for 2 minutes, until golden, them remove and drain on paper towels. Continue with the rest of the vegetables. Season them generously with salt and serve with the yogurt dip, topped with the remaining mint leaves and lemon wedges for squeezing on the side.

DINNER
DÎNER

DINNER IN ST. TROPEZ feels like a feast every night. During the sunset golden hour, people begin to flock into town, weaving around the cobbled streets. During the busy summer months the restaurant kitchens are blazing with grilled langoustines, charred entrecôte and buttery baked sea bass with traditional *tomates provençals* or *légumes farcis* on the side. For me, the ultimate dinner destination is in the old town, where there are three restaurants that for decades have evoked the very essence of St. Tropez food. These are all huddled together on the rue des Remparts: La Ponche, La Pesquière and Le Mazagran. According to Madame Duckstein herself, whose family bought La Ponche in 1938, Brigitte Bardot once said that this spot was the most romantic place in town. I could not agree more.

I can't write about dinner without mentioning my grandmother Bubi. She first introduced me to seafood in Port Grimaud at La Table du Mareyeur. Every summer Bubi lived to come to this family-run business, where towering platters of lobster, tiger prawns, clams and oysters make up their spectacular *fruits de mer* menu. This is how seafood should be: simple and rich in color with lashings of lemon juice. One of my earliest memories is of Bubi attacking one of these magnificent platters wearing a bib, with both hands dripping in gold jewelry. She made something so messy look ridiculously elegant!

Dinner parties with my family and friends are perhaps the best of all. Alongside the tempting cooking smells wafting from the neighbors' kitchen, dinnertime on La Giscle carries the sound of chinking glasses, the last few boats chugging away—usually from our house—and Martha and the Vandellas' "Heatwave." Donatella's Saffron Risotto with Duck Liver, my Crab Pasta on the Rocks and Steak à la Nina can be created with minimal effort, and have all been happily devoured many times right here in my back garden.

POLENTA VERTE AUX COEURS D'ARTICHAUTS | GREEN POLENTA WITH ARTICHOKE HEARTS

SERVES 2

1¾ cups (6½ oz/200 g) fresh or frozen shelled fava beans

⅔ cup (3½ oz/100 g) fresh or frozen peas

scant ½ cup (3 oz/90 g) quick-cook polenta

2 cups (16 fl oz/500 ml) hot vegetable stock

scant 1 cup (3½ oz/100 g) freshly grated Parmesan, plus extra for serving

handful fresh flat-leaf parsley leaves

handful fresh mint leaves

6 preserved artichoke hearts in oil, drained

1–2 tbsp extra-virgin olive oil

sea salt and black pepper

As well as being sensational in sweet things, polenta is a light, healthy, gluten-free savory option, and this dinner will take you no more than 15 minutes to make. Polenta is a type of ground cornmeal that's often described as a peasant food and is unbeatable with chanterelles, when they're in season, or in this dish.

Bring a large pan of salted water to a boil, add the fava beans and cook for 3 minutes, then add the peas and cook for another 2 minutes. Drain and set aside. In the same saucepan, over medium-high heat, pour in the polenta and the stock and stir with a wooden spoon. It will thicken quickly, but continue to cook, stirring constantly, until it bubbles, then remove from heat. Mix in the grated Parmesan. Chop most of the parsley and mint leaves and add to the polenta, then season with salt and pepper. Spoon onto two plates, then top with the fava beans and peas. Place the artichoke hearts on top and finish with the reserved mint and parsley leaves and a drizzle of extra-virgin olive oil. Serve immediately.

LÉGUMES FARCIS 'LE MISTRAL' | LE MISTRAL STUFFED VEGETABLES

MAKES 8

2 eggplants
2 zucchini
4 tomatoes
2 tbsp olive oil
1 shallot, finely diced
3 cloves garlic, finely diced
1 tbsp chopped fresh sage
1 tbsp chopped fresh rosemary
½ lb (250 g) ground beef
1 can (13 oz/400 g) plum tomatoes
2 pinches of sugar
1⅓ cups (5 oz/150 g) dried
sourdough bread crumbs
sour cream, to serve (optional)
sea salt and black pepper

Stuffed vegetables make a welcome starter or side, and this recipe is so versatile that you can use all types of vegetables. I fondly remember eating these with my family at La Pesquière restaurant during the Mistral, the strong wind that affects the south of France.

Slice the eggplants in half lengthwise and use a spoon to scrape out the flesh into a bowl. Season the inside of the skins generously with salt and set aside. Prepare the zucchini in the same way and set aside with the eggplants. Using a small knife, carefully cut around the tomato stems, pry away the tops and reserve. Use a teaspoon to scoop out the center, letting the juices and seeds fall into the bowl. Pat the eggplant skins dry with paper towels. Line a baking pan with parchment paper, add a little olive oil and spread it around the pan. Place all the vegetables, cut side up, in the pan.

Preheat the oven to 400°F (200°C). Heat a splash of olive oil in a large frying pan over medium heat. Add the shallot and cook, stirring, until translucent. Add the garlic and herbs and allow the flavors to merge for a moment. Mash the scooped-out vegetable flesh with a knife and add to the pan. Increase the heat a little and add the beef, breaking it up a little and letting it brown. Stir in the plum tomatoes and sugar and season with salt and pepper, then bring to a boil. Reduce the heat and simmer for 15-20 minutes, or until the sauce has thickened and reduced by one-third. Taste to check for seasoning. Spoon the sauce into the vegetable cases, filling each one to the top. Sprinkle generously with bread crumbs. Put the tomato stems alongside the filled vegetables and bake everything for about 40 minutes, or until they look slightly shriveled and lovely and golden. You may need to remove the tomato stems after 10-15 minutes to stop them from burning. To serve, arrange the vegetables on serving plates and place the tomato stems on top of the stuffed tomatoes. Serve hot, at room temperature or cold, with a dollop of sour cream, if you like.

PÂTES À LA FAÇON DE CHEZ BRUNO | PASTA IN THE SPIRIT OF CHEZ BRUNO

SERVES 2

2 tbsp olive oil
½ lb (250 g) cremini mushrooms, sliced
6½ oz (200 g) dried tagliatelle
2 cloves garlic, finely diced
⅔ cup (3½ oz/100 g) cooked chestnuts, chopped
2 tbsp roughly chopped fresh chives
1 tbsp crème fraîche
2 tbsp truffle oil
Comté cheese, grated, to serve
sea salt and black pepper

Chez Bruno is a magical and unusual family-run restaurant in Lorgues. After wandering through the giant truffle sculptures, you are greeted by a garden and hotel in the style of a grand old vineyard, designed by Bruno himself. In the spirit of Chez Bruno, I have used truffle oil and other earthy flavors from chestnuts and mushrooms. If you are lucky enough to get your hands on a truffle, go ahead and swap it for the mushrooms and then grate over as much as you like.

Bring a large pan of salted water to a boil. While it heats up, heat the olive oil in a large frying pan, add the mushrooms and cook until they have shrunk in size by about half. Cook the tagliatelle for about 10 minutes, or until al dente (check the instructions on the package). Add the garlic to the mushrooms and let it cook for a moment before adding the chestnuts and seasoning generously with salt and pepper. Ladle in three spoonfuls of the pasta cooking water. Drain the tagliatelle and add it to the pan. Add the chives, crème fraîche and truffle oil and taste to check the seasoning. Sprinkle with cheese and serve immediately.

AUBERGINES ET TOMATES AU QUATRE ÉPICES DE LA PLACE DES LICES

LA PLACE DES LICES'S EGGPLANT AND TOMATO WITH QUATRE ÉPICES

SERVES 4 AS A SIDE DISH OR STARTER

2 eggplants, sliced
⅜ inch (1 cm) thick
2–3 tbsp olive oil
1 clove garlic, thinly sliced
1 can (13 oz/400 g) plum tomatoes
scant ½ tsp superfine sugar
½ tsp quatre épices (see below)
fresh basil leaves, to garnish
2 tbsp extra-virgin olive oil
sea salt and black pepper

FOR THE QUATRE ÉPICES
1 tsp ground cinnamon
1 tsp ground nutmeg
1 tsp ground cloves
1–2 tsp black pepper

Many restaurants out here serve this dish as a side or a starter, and they all vary a little depending on where you are. With vegetables bought from La Place des Lices market, my version uses a four-spice blend called quatre épices, often found at local French stores, which consists of ground cinnamon, cloves, pepper and nutmeg. Sometimes ginger is used instead of cinnamon, but either way the blend is widely used in French and Middle Eastern kitchens.

Preheat the oven to 375°F (190°C) and line a sheet pan with parchment paper. Put the eggplant slices on paper towels, season generously with salt and leave for a few minutes. Meanwhile, put the spices for the quatre épices into a jar and shake. Set aside. Now, heat some olive oil in a frying pan over medium-high heat, add the sliced garlic and sizzle for 1 minute. Once the garlic begins to color lightly, add the tomatoes, sugar and quatre épices and break the tomatoes up with a wooden spoon. Bring to a boil, then turn down to a gentle simmer until thickened and reduced by about a third.

Wipe any liquid from the eggplants with paper towels, season with the remaining olive oil and pepper and place the circles neatly in rows on the prepared pan. Bake for about 25 minutes, until tender. Taste the tomatoes to check the seasoning and remove from the heat. Spoon the tomato sauce generously over the eggplant slices. Don't worry if sauce spills over—you're going for the rustic look! Bake the slices again for 25 minutes, or until they look lovely and golden and the tomato sauce has set into them. Use a slotted spatula to transfer them to a serving platter and then top with basil leaves and a last drizzle of extra-virgin olive oil. Eat hot or cold. These are also great the next day.

TOMATES À LA PROVENÇAL | PROVENÇAL TOMATOES

SERVES 4

These are usually eaten with meat or grilled fish, for lunch or dinner. They're delicious hot or cold.

2 slices stale sourdough bread
2 large tomatoes
1 clove garlic
few sprigs fresh rosemary
1 tsp herbes de Provence
2 tbsp olive oil
sea salt and black pepper

Preheat the oven to 375°F (190°C) and line a sheet pan with parchment paper. Cut the bread into chunks and bake for 20 minutes, then remove and blitz in a blender to bread crumb consistency.

Halve the tomatoes widthwise and grate the garlic over the cut halves. Carefully press the rosemary sprigs into the tomatoes so that the leaves are sticking out like small palm trees. Sprinkle the herbes de Provence on top and season with salt and pepper. Sprinkle with the bread crumbs. Arrange on the sheet pan and drizzle olive oil over the halves. Bake for about 40 minutes, or until the sides have shriveled and the tops are crispy.

GRATIN DE FENOUIL ET CAROTTE À LA MUSCADE | FENNEL, CARROT AND NUTMEG GRATIN

SERVES 4 AS A SIDE DISH

4 tbsp olive oil, plus extra
for greasing
2 fennel bulbs, sliced
¼ inch (5 mm) thick
1 yellow onion, thinly sliced
6½ oz (200 g) carrots,
sliced ¼ inch (5 mm) thick
2 cloves garlic, diced
freshly grated nutmeg
2 tbsp fresh thyme leaves
½ tsp sea salt
1¼ cups (10 fl oz/300 ml)
whole milk
6½ tbsp (3½ fl oz/100 ml)
heavy cream
1 tbsp sourdough bread crumbs
black pepper

A welcome change from the famous gratin dauphinois, this is particularly good with steak. You can assemble the vegetables in the baking dish the night before and cook the next day at your leisure.

Preheat the oven to 400°F (200°C) and grease a 12 x 20-inch (30 x 50-cm) baking dish. Put the vegetables in a mixing bowl, add the garlic, nutmeg, thyme and olive oil and season well with the salt and some pepper. Toss the vegetables to make sure everything is coated and well mixed. Make a layer of fennel and onions in the bottom of the baking dish, then top with a layer of carrots and finish with a layer of fennel and onions. Pack the dish down well, filling in all the gaps. Mix together the milk and cream. Bake for 1 hour and 15 minutes, then remove and pour over enough milk and cream mixture to leave about ¼ inch (5 mm) uncovered. Sprinkle the bread crumbs on top and return to the oven for another 15 minutes, until the top is beautifully golden. Check if the gratin is cooked by inserting a sharp knife; if the knife slips in easily, it is ready. Serve immediately.

CREVETTES TIGRÉES DE BUBI | BUBI'S TIGER PRAWNS

SERVES 4

2 tbsp olive oil
2 tsp unsalted butter
3 cloves garlic, finely diced
pinch of dried chile flakes,
plus extra for sprinkling
10 oz (320 g) raw tiger or
jumbo king prawns
2 tbsp Calvados
2 tbsp chopped fresh chives
bunch fresh flat-leaf parsley,
roughly chopped
1 batch Aïoli (page 90) or
good-quality mayonnaise
(optional)
sea salt and black pepper

My grandmother Bubi's favorite place in the world was La Table du Mareyeur, a popular seafood restaurant that holds many great memories for my family. Tucked away under one of Port Grimaud's little bridges, it owes its success to the welcoming owners, Ewan and Caroline. Bubi dined here many times. I have included this great prawn recipe in her memory and as a nod to the giant prawns that are always a favorite on the menu at La Table du Mareyeur. It's perfect for a starter with a crunchy fresh salad.

Place a large frying pan over medium-high heat. Add the oil and butter, and once it is hot, add the garlic and chile flakes. Let the flavors infuse for a moment before adding the prawns. Shake the prawns in the pan, frying until one side is golden before turning them over. They will take 4–5 minutes in total. During the final minute of cooking, add the Calvados and sprinkle with the chopped herbs. Season well with salt and pepper, and they're ready to eat. If using, sprinkle the Aïoli or mayonnaise with chile flakes and serve alongside.

PÂTES AU CRABE SUR LES ROCHERS | CRAB PASTA ON THE ROCKS

SERVES 4

2 crabs, live or cooked
(or 13 oz/400 g crabmeat)
13 oz (400 g) spaghetti
1 tbsp grated fresh ginger
3 cloves garlic, finely diced
1 shallot, very finely diced
½ cup (3½ oz/100 g) cherry
tomatoes, halved
1½ tsp superfine sugar
finely grated zest and juice of
4 limes
large bunch fresh cilantro,
roughly chopped
bunch fresh chives,
finely chopped
4 tbsp (2 fl oz/60 ml)
extra-virgin olive oil
sea salt and black pepper

This party pasta dish always makes an appearance at birthdays and large dinners out here. It looks stunning on the plate and has seaside written all over it. Of course, you can buy the crabmeat, but apart from cooking the pasta, there's little else to do, so it's worth having a go at picking your own crab.

If using live crabs, bring a large pot of water to a boil, drop in the crabs, and cook for about 15 minutes. Remove from the pot and let cool. To pick a crab, you'll need a cutting board, two clean tea towels, a clean hammer, two bowls and a crab picker. Pull off all the legs and claws and set aside. Place one tea towel on the cutting board, one of the crab bodies on top and the other tea towel on top of the crab. Use the hammer to crack the top so you can pick out the crabmeat into one of the bowls and discard the body in the second bowl. Pick any meat that may be left where the claws were pulled into the bowl with the rest of the meat. Do the same with the other body. Now, using the technique of covering with the tea towel and hammering, do the same with the claws and legs, being careful not to hit them too vigorously to avoid getting too much shell mixed in with the meat. Use a crab picker to extract every last bit from inside the legs and claws. Once finished, check through the meat for any leftover shell and remember that inside each crab claw there is always a large piece of cartilage that must be discarded.

Cook the spaghetti according to the package instructions. Put all the remaining ingredients, including the crabmeat, in a large mixing bowl and lightly toss them together. When the pasta is cooked, scoop out a cup of the cooking water, then drain the pasta. Add the pasta to the mixing bowl and stir well, pouring in a little of the cooking water to loosen it. Taste to check for seasoning and add more salt and pepper if needed. Serve immediately.

TARTINE DE NOIX DE SAINT-JACQUES ET SAUCE AUX TOMATES, POIS CHICHES ET PIMENT

SCALLOP TARTINE WITH TOMATO, CHICKPEA AND CHILE SAUCE

SERVES 2

1 tbsp olive oil
4 cloves garlic, diced
3 anchovy fillets, chopped
good pinch of dried chile flakes
1 can (13 oz/400 g) plum tomatoes
½ cup (3½ oz/100 g) rinsed and
drained canned chickpeas
½ tsp sugar
4 slices sourdough bread
1 tsp unsalted butter
6½ oz (200 g) scallops
1 lemon, cut into wedges
bunch fresh basil
1 tbsp extra-virgin olive oil
sea salt and black pepper

In the local beach restaurants, scallops are usually cooked in a shamelessly garlicky sauce with a gratin on top, and you can do something similar by spooning on a teaspoon of my Persillade, opposite. The alternative is this tartine, which uses pantry staples and turns them into an attractive, healthy dinner with a kick.

Heat the olive oil in a large frying pan with two-thirds of the garlic and the anchovy fillets and let them melt together for a minute or two before adding the chile flakes. Pour in the tomatoes and chickpeas and bring to a boil, breaking up the tomatoes with a wooden spoon. Lower the heat to a simmer and reduce by about half. Season with sugar, salt and pepper and leave to simmer gently.

Preheat the broiler and toast the sourdough slices under it. Heat the butter in another frying pan, add the remaining garlic, and once the garlic is sizzling, add the scallops to brown for 3 minutes, turning them over halfway. Season the scallops with black pepper and a squeeze of lemon juice. Place the toast on two serving plates. Tear the basil into the sauce, reserving a few whole leaves, and generously spoon the sauce, followed by the scallops, onto the toasted sourdough. Scatter with the basil leaves and a drizzle of extra-virgin olive oil. Serve with lemon wedges.

PERSILLADE

**MAKES ABOUT ½ CUP
(1¾-2 OZ/50-60 G)**

1 small clove garlic
2 large bunches fresh
flat-leaf parsley
few drops lemon juice
2-3 tbsp extra-virgin olive oil
sea salt and black pepper

I use this on everything and anything: in dressings, on baked fish, as a dip with toasted bread, or simply spooned onto fresh scallops and then baked in a hot oven for 5-6 minutes. For even more depth of flavor you could add anchovy fillets and omit the salt. A little goes a long way.

Mash the garlic and a pinch of salt to a paste with a mortar and pestle. Remove the stems from the parsley and save them for a stock. Chop the leaves to a very fine, green mass, roughly 6 tablespoons in total. Mix with the garlic paste and add the lemon juice, olive oil and some pepper. It should be of spreading consistency and have a sharp garlic and parsley tang. Keeps in the fridge for up to 5 days.

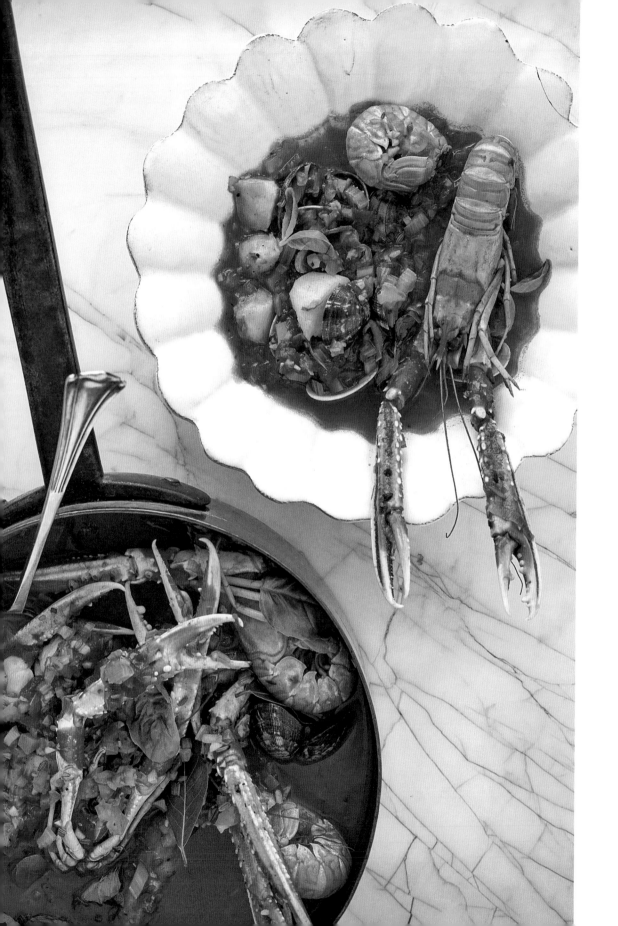

LA BOUILLABAISSE DE MONSIEUR JACQUES FÉLINE | JACQUES FÉLINE'S BOUILLABAISSE

SERVES 4 AS A MAIN COURSE OR 6 AS A STARTER

2 tbsp olive oil
1 onion, diced
2 small shallots, diced
1 celery heart, diced
1 carrot, diced
1 leek, chopped
10 cloves garlic, diced
1 tbsp fresh thyme leaves
1 tbsp chopped fresh rosemary
2 tsp fennel seeds
few juniper berries
2 bay leaves
2 tbsp tomato purée
1 can (28 oz/875 g) plum tomatoes
1 vegetable stock cube, dissolved in 2½ qt (2.5 l) boiling water
pinch of saffron threads
6–8 langoustines
1 lb (500 g) clams, scrubbed clean
10 oz (300 g) monkfish fillet, cut into ¾-inch (2-cm) chunks
finely grated zest and juice of 1 unwaxed lemon
finely grated zest of 1 orange
small bunch fresh chives, chopped
handful fresh basil leaves
sea salt and black pepper

Jacques Féline often tells the story of how he makes his authentic rustic version of bouillabaisse: he goes fishing on his boat, catches an assortment of fish and crushes the clam and mussel shells to a fine rubble that he later adds to the stock. He leaves the stock for two days to infuse and develop the fishy flavor before straining it. My version isn't quite as romantic, and it doesn't take as long! Traditionally, bouillabaisse uses at least six different kinds of shellfish and fish. It was a peasant dish for which the leftover catch was thrown into the pot, including the well-known rascasse (scorpion fish). You can use any fish or shellfish you like. The only rule is that you need at least one scaly fish and one with a shell to give a varied seafood flavor. It's a spectacular dinner party feast, so make sure you have an occasion for it!

Heat the olive oil in a large saucepan over medium-high heat. Add the onion and shallots and cook gently until translucent before adding the rest of the vegetables and herbs. Stir well, making sure everything is coated in the flavors. Add the tomato purée and plum tomatoes, followed by the vegetable stock and saffron. Bring to a boil for 2 minutes, then reduce the heat and simmer for 1½ hours.

Bring the sauce back up to a boil, add the langoustines and cook for 6 minutes. Add the clams and cook for 4 more minutes, then add the monkfish and continue to cook for another 2 minutes. Remove from the heat, add the citrus zest and juice and season with salt and pepper. Stir in the chives and basil, reserving a little basil to garnish. Taste and check the seasoning, then serve, sprinkled with basil.

CARRELET MEUNIÈRE AU THYM ET AUX AMANDES | PLAICE MEUNIÈRE WITH THYME AND ALMONDS

SERVES 2

scant ½ cup (2½ oz/70 g)
all-purpose flour
2 plaice fillets
2 tsp unsalted butter
1 tbsp olive oil
few sprigs fresh thyme,
leaves picked
1 clove garlic, diced
2½ tbsp blanched almonds, halved
½ lemon, cut into wedges,
to serve
sea salt and black pepper

The French usually use lemon sole when cooking meunière-style—that is, dredged in flour and fried in butter—but any other flatfish will do. Plaice, a European flounder, is cheap, superfast to panfry and soaks up flavors beautifully. It's delicious with Provençal Tomatoes (page 161).

Put the flour in a shallow bowl and season with salt and pepper. Dip the fillets into the flour, making sure every last bit is coated. Dust off any excess flour and place a large frying pan over medium-high heat. Once the pan is hot, add the butter and olive oil and allow to melt and sizzle. Place the fish fillets in the hot pan and fry for 2 minutes before carefully turning them over with tongs to cook for a further 2 minutes. After turning the fillets, add the thyme leaves, garlic and almonds and move everything around the pan so that the almonds and garlic begin to color. Serve immediately, with a final squeeze of lemon.

MAQUEREAU POCHÉ À L'HUILE D'OLIVE ET FREEKEH | MACKEREL POACHED IN OLIVE OIL WITH FREEKEH

SERVES 2

1 cup (5 oz/150 g) freekeh
1¾ cups (14 fl oz/450 ml) water
⅓ cup (1¾ oz/50 g) raisins
1 tbsp pumpkin seeds
½ cup (3½ oz/100 g) cherry tomatoes, chopped
bunch fresh flat-leaf parsley, chopped
1 small shallot, diced
2 mackerel fillets
5 black peppercorns
1 bay leaf
1 tsp fennel seeds
pared rind and juice of ½ unwaxed lemon
about 1¼ cups (10 fl oz/300 ml) olive oil
sea salt and black pepper

This is a great way to lock in the precious omega-3 fats found in mackerel, and it's one of the first techniques I learned when I was working in restaurants. It's served with freekeh, a type of green wheat that is unbelievably good for you. I use an inexpensive olive oil when poaching, and always strain and keep the oil to reuse for other fish dishes.

Put the freekeh, water and a good pinch of salt in a saucepan, stir and bring to a boil. Cover with a lid and reduce the heat to a simmer for about 25 minutes, or until the freekeh is tender. It should retain a little bite and have doubled in size. Drain and transfer to a serving bowl along with the raisins, pumpkin seeds, tomatoes, parsley and shallot. Toss together and season with salt, pepper, lemon juice and a splash of olive oil.

Meanwhile, preheat the oven to 325°F (170°C). Use tweezers to remove any visible bones from the mackerel fillets and place them in a small baking dish they can lie flat in. Add the peppercorns, bay leaf, fennel seeds, lemon rind and some salt, then pour the olive oil over the mackerel until it is just covered. Cut a piece of parchment paper to the size of the baking dish and place on top of the fish so that it is just touching the oil. Bake for 15–18 minutes, until the fillets appear pink in color and the olive oil has started bubbling on the surface. Carefully lift the fillets out of the oil, letting the excess drip off, and discard the peppercorns and lemon rind. Serve the fish with the freekeh and a last squeeze of lemon.

ROUGET BARBET À L'ACQUA PAZZA DU PÊCHEUR | FISHERMAN'S CRAZY WATER RED MULLET

SERVES 2

1 red mullet or other delicately
flavored white-fleshed fish,
cleaned
2 tbsp olive oil
few sprigs fresh rosemary
1 unwaxed lemon, ½ sliced
and ½ for serving
5 cloves garlic, sliced
2 anchovy fillets
1–2 pinches of dried chile flakes
¼ cup (1¾ oz/50 g) cherry
tomatoes, halved
3 tbsp (1¼ oz/40 g) black olives,
pitted
2 tbsp red wine
6½ tbsp (3½ fl oz/100 ml)
seawater or Badoit mineral water
handful fresh basil leaves
sea salt and black pepper

In the south of France, red mullet is usually a mistake catch for a fisherman, so they're not often available. But if you spot one, you must buy it and try this. You won't be disappointed. Ridiculously simple and tasty, it not only looks stunning with its flaming pink skin, but this quirky cooking method also makes it very special. Ask the fishmonger to leave in the liver, as it has a unique creamy texture that must be tried. If you can't lay your hands on any seawater from the bay of St. Tropez, Badoit mineral water will also do the job! I like this dish with potatoes roasted with rosemary.

Heat a griddle pan over medium-high heat. Season the fish with olive oil, salt and pepper and tuck the rosemary and a few lemon slices into the fish's cavity. Place the fish on the griddle for 1½ minutes until lovely and golden, then turn over and cook for another 2 minutes. Move the fish at least once on each side to avoid it sticking to the pan and breaking the skin. Set aside.

Heat a splash of olive oil in a frying pan large enough to hold the fish over medium-high heat. Once the oil is hot, add the garlic and anchovies. Break up the anchovies with a wooden spoon and allow them to melt down for 2 minutes before adding the chile flakes, tomatoes and olives. Stir well and carefully place the mullet on top. Pour over the red wine, followed by the sea- or mineral water, and let bubble for 1–2 minutes to burn off the alcohol. Cover with a lid and cook for about 10 minutes, until the flesh begins to flake away from the bones. Taste to check the seasoning, then transfer the fish to a serving plate, drizzle with the sauce and tumble the basil leaves on top. Serve immediately.

SARDINES DE LUCIEN | LUCIEN'S SARDINES

SERVES 4

2 tbsp olive oil
4 small shallots, diced
8 sardine fillets
3 cloves garlic, diced
6½ tbsp (3½ fl oz/100 ml)
white wine
⅓ cup (1¾ oz/50 g) raisins
1 green onion, chopped
¼ cup (1¼ oz/40 g) pine nuts,
toasted
handful fresh flat-leaf parsley,
chopped
sea salt and black pepper

My buddy Lucien is a fisherman and he lives in St. Tropez. Most mornings at 7am, he moors his beautifully rustic boat in line with the other classic wooden fishing boats at the front of the harbor. He then has a coffee and chats with his mate in a café overlooking the bay. I have been lucky to have been out on his boat a few times; it is not only the oldest boat in the harbor but it was once owned by Brigitte Bardot herself. He tells me that these Provençal griddled sardines are the St. Tropez fisherman's favorite. Ask the fishmonger to fillet the sardines for you. They're even better on the barbecue.

Heat the olive oil in a large frying pan, add the shallots and cook over low heat until soft and translucent. Meanwhile, place a griddle pan over medium-high heat and season the sardine fillets all over with olive oil, pepper and a little salt (the sardines are naturally salty). Once the pan is hot, add 4 fillets, skin side down, and leave to char for about 4 minutes. Carefully move with a slotted spatula halfway through to prevent them from sticking to the pan. Once the skins have charred, remove the fillets and set aside. Repeat with the remaining fillets. By now the shallots should have wilted and reduced by half. Add the garlic and let it cook for a few minutes, then add the sardines and increase the heat. Pour over the white wine and let the juices simmer and infuse, then add the remaining ingredients. Simmer for 2–3 minutes, until the fish begins to flake. Serve immediately, or eat at room temperature. *Pas mal!*

LOUP EN PAPILLOTE POUR UN BARBECUE SUR LA PLAGE | BARBECUE ON THE BEACH WITH SEA BASS PARCELS

SERVES 2

2 tbsp olive oil
1 tsp unsalted butter
1 large fennel bulb, thinly sliced
2 banana shallots or 5–6 regular shallots, thinly sliced
3 cloves garlic, diced
2 whole sea bass, cleaned and gutted
2 tsp honey
2 tbsp white wine
1 lemon, sliced
small bunch flat-leaf parsley
sea salt and black pepper

I like to prepare the fish at home by wrapping it with the fillings in aluminum foil, then pedal down to the beach with it in a picnic basket on my bike, along with a couple of bottles of chilled rosé. My friend Jean-Baptiste and his friends have usually organized a blazing barbecue on our little local beach. The fish goes straight onto the roaring grill and we make a start on the wine while it cooks. This dish is particularly good served alongside the Géant Casino Tabbouleh (page 52).

Preheat the oven to 400°F (200°C) or light the barbecue. Cut two sheets of parchment paper and two sheets of aluminum foil large enough to cover the fish. Heat the olive oil and butter in a large frying pan until hot. Add the fennel and shallots and cook for a few minutes, until softened. When they begin to brown, add the garlic and stir together for a moment, then remove from the heat.

Lay out the sheets of foil with the parchment paper on top (this prevents the fish from piercing the parcel). Divide the onion and fennel mixture between the two pieces of paper and place a sea bass on top of each. Season with salt and pepper. Fold in the ends of each parcel on either side of the fish's head and tail and gradually begin to tightly twist it into a sealed package, leaving a 4-inch (10-cm) hole open at the top. Distribute the honey, white wine, lemon slices and parsley equally between the parcels before sealing the tops. Tightly fold the foil under the fish to make a tight and compact parcel. Place the foil packages on a sheet pan and bake for about 45 minutes, or grill on a preheated barbecue, covered, for 30 minutes. The fish should be perfectly cooked and tender. Serve in the foil packages for guests to open at the table.

SAUMON POUR CÉDRIC | CÉDRIC'S SALMON

SERVES 2

3½ oz (100 g) green beans
3½ oz (10 g) sugar snap peas
½ cup (2½ oz/80 g) fresh or
frozen peas
1 red Belgian endive
½ red onion, diced
1 tbsp avocado oil
2 salmon fillet steaks
(about ½ lb/260 g in total)
finely grated zest and juice of
1 unwaxed lemon, plus wedges
to serve
6–8 fresh basil leaves
1⅓ cups (1¼ oz/40 g)
arugula leaves
sea salt and black pepper

FOR THE DRESSING
3 tbsp avocado oil
1 tbsp balsamic vinegar
1 tsp Dijon mustard
½ tsp English mustard
sea salt and black pepper

This is my brother Adam's recipe. Cédric is a superfit tennis coach who works at the local club in Cogolin, and is quite an amazing individual, always bursting with energy and enthusiasm. He claims his energy levels are thanks to his fuss-free diet of fruit and vegetables and heaps of walking. I gave him this recipe last time I saw him, and he gave it the Cédric seal of approval. In other words, it's gold!

Preheat the oven to 400°F (200°C) and line a sheet pan with parchment paper. Bring a saucepan of water to a boil and add the green beans and sugar snap peas. Cook for 5 minutes, then add the peas and boil for another 2 minutes, then drain. Slice the endive lengthwise into 6 wedges. Put the diced onion in a sieve under cold running water for a few seconds.

Heat a drop of avocado oil in a nonstick frying pan over medium heat. Season the salmon fillets with salt and pepper. Carefully make three or four incisions at an angle about halfway into each fillet. Fill them with lemon zest and a whole basil leaf. Place the fillets in the hot pan and fry for about 2–3 minutes, until the skin is crisp, then transfer to the sheet pan. Bake for 4–5 minutes for rare (it will cook more quickly than usual because of the incisions).

While the salmon cooks, mix together the ingredients for the dressing and toss two-thirds of it with the vegetables and arugula leaves in a bowl. Taste to check the seasoning.

Divide the vegetables equally into serving bowls and carefully balance a salmon fillet on top of each. Drizzle the remaining dressing around the plate, add a squeeze of lemon and serve with extra wedges. Voilà!

POULET À L'ESTRAGON, CHAMPIGNONS ET POIS CHICHES | TARRAGON CHICKEN WITH MUSHROOMS AND CHICKPEAS

SERVES 4

3 tbsp olive oil

8 chicken thighs, bone in

3 banana shallots or 8–9 regular shallots, thinly sliced

2 cups (13 oz/400 g) rinsed and drained canned chickpeas

13 oz (400 g) fresh chanterelle mushrooms, halved

2 star anise

3 cloves garlic, sliced

bunch fresh thyme, leaves picked

3 batches Tarragon Dressing (page 59)

sea salt and black pepper

Poulet à l'estragon is an all-time classic in the south of France, and in restaurants it usually comes in a creamy mushroom sauce. To make it a little lighter and fresher, I just drizzle over my simple tarragon dressing at the end. Chicken thighs on the bone, as opposed to breasts, are far more flavorful, and the vegetables soak up all the delicious meat juices while frying in the pan.

Heat 2 tablespoons of the oil in a large saucepan over medium-high heat. Season the chicken thighs generously with olive oil, salt and pepper and add to the hot pan, skin side down. Cook for about 6 minutes, until the skins are golden brown, moving them once with tongs to keep them from sticking to the pan. Turn them over, add the shallots and stir. Add the chickpeas, mushrooms and star anise and allow the mushrooms to reduce in volume by half, then turn the thighs back to skin side down. Add the garlic and thyme and let everything infuse for a few moments. The chicken should be cooked through after about 15 minutes in total; the juice should run clear when a thigh is pierced with a knife. Remove the star anise and serve with the dressing drizzled on top.

SOURIS D'AGNEAU, ANCHOIS ET ÉPICES | LAMB SHANKS WITH ANCHOVY AND SPICES

SERVES 4

4 lamb shanks
4 tbsp olive oil
2 tbsp peanut oil
4 cloves garlic, sliced
8 anchovy fillets
2 tsp coriander seeds
2 tsp cumin seeds
2 tsp ground sumac
2 tsp fennel seeds
bunch fresh rosemary
sea salt and black pepper

Although it might seem strange, it's typically Provençal to use anchovies with roast lamb; these little fish are a wonderful secret ingredient. During the slow cooking, the fish flavor melts down into the sauce to add another dimension that works unbelievably well with the lamb. It's a great dish for a dinner party. These lamb shanks are fantastic with the Géant Casino Tabbouleh (page 52).

Preheat the oven to 300°F (150°C). Season the lamb shanks with a little olive oil, salt and pepper and heat the peanut oil in a large frying pan until hot. Add the shanks and cook for 7 minutes to brown the meat on all sides, turning it with tongs. Tear 8 pieces of aluminum foil large enough to cover each shank, a little larger than letter-size. Lay out 4 pieces on the work surface and place a shank in the middle of each sheet. Divide the garlic, anchovies and spices equally among the shanks and season again with the remaining olive oil, salt and pepper. Wrap the meat tightly into packages, sealing and closing up any gaps. This is important, as you want the lamb to cook in its own juices, and any gaps could cause it to dry out. Use the last four sheets of foil to make a second layer around each parcel. Place the parcels in a roasting pan.

Roast the shanks for 3 hours, without opening the parcels. After cooking, carefully unwrap the parcels and pour the juices into a saucepan. Set the lamb shanks aside and keep warm. Simmer the juices for a few minutes over high heat to reduce and thicken. Serve the sauce over the lamb shanks and eat immediately.

RAGOÛT DE LAPIN DE GASSIN | GASSIN'S RABBIT CASSEROLE

SERVES 4

2 whole rabbits
(about 3 lb/1.6 kg meat)
4 tbsp olive oil
9½ oz (300 g) lardons
8 small shallots, diced
8 cloves garlic, diced
bunch fresh thyme
3 bay leaves
⅔–¾ cup (5–6½ fl oz/150–200 ml)
white wine
4 baby fennel bulbs, quartered
lengthwise
2 carrots, quartered lengthwise
4 cans (13 oz/400 g each) plum
tomatoes
12 baby pickled onions
¾ cup (3½ oz/100 g) pistachios,
roughly chopped
handful chopped fresh cilantro
sea salt and black pepper

When I worked at L'Anima restaurant in London, they served a mouth-watering Sicilian rabbit dish that was covered in pickled onions, black olives and pistachios. Now I have grown to love the French version, so my lapin Provençal takes the best from both the French and Italian dishes. I've named this Gassin's Rabbit Casserole because when I first made it I used a white wine from one of the local Gassin vineyards. It's fantastic served with long-grain brown rice. If rabbit's not your cup of tea, use bone-in chicken thighs or a large whole chicken and adjust the timings accordingly.

Ask the butcher to cut each rabbit into 8 pieces. Season the meat with salt, pepper and olive oil. Heat a large frying pan over medium-high heat, add the rabbit pieces in batches and brown on all sides, then remove and set aside. Meanwhile, heat half the olive oil in a saucepan large enough to fit all the ingredients over medium-high heat. Once the oil is hot, add the lardons and cook until golden. Remove and set aside, then add the shallots and cook gently until softened and translucent. Add the garlic, fried lardons, rabbit pieces, thyme and bay leaves and stir well. Increase the heat, pour over the white wine and let it bubble for a few minutes to burn off the alcohol.

Add the fennel and carrots to the pan. Add the plum tomatoes, breaking them up with a wooden spoon and stirring well. Fill the tomato cans with water and pour over just enough water to cover the rabbit, then bring to a boil. Reduce the heat and simmer for about 3 hours, or until the meat gently falls off the bone. During the last 20 minutes, stir in the pickled onions, then taste to check the seasoning. Just before serving, sprinkle with the chopped pistachios and cilantro.

CANARD RÔTI AU VIN ROUGE FAÇON LA VERDOYANTE | RUBY RED ROASTED DUCK LA VERDOYANTE STYLE

SERVES 4

8 Black Mission figs, halved
1⅓ cups (11 fl oz/350 ml) red wine
1 whole duck
7 tbsp (3½ oz/100 g)
unsalted butter
6–7 slices bacon
4 cloves garlic, roughly chopped
few sprigs fresh thyme
⅔ cup (3½ oz/100 g) cooked
chestnuts, halved
sea salt and black pepper

La Verdoyante in Gassin is a restaurant run by two generations of the Mouret family. It's on a farm with one of the best views on the coast. I've been going there for years, and when I was little I used to chase the chickens and ducks around the farm behind the house. It was my paradise then, but these days I'd probably be chasing them for a not-so-sweet reason. Chef Laurent often brings old, unheard-of French dishes like this one back to life. I serve it with mashed potatoes with parsnips and blanched asparagus for a dramatic contrast of colors. Something as dark and silky as this roast needs a showstopper of a dessert, so try my La Môle's Marbled Chocolate Mousse (page 231). Boom!

Preheat the oven to 350°F (180°C) and line a roasting pan with parchment paper. Put the figs in a bowl with the red wine and leave to soak for 30 minutes. Grease the duck with half the butter and season generously with salt and pepper. Layer the bacon over the duck, which will stop it from drying out and will add extra flavor while roasting. Stuff half the garlic and half the soaked figs into the bird's cavity. Roast for 40 minutes, then remove and add the remaining figs, butter and garlic. Stick the thyme into the cavity and pour over the wine. Bake for about 1 more hour, basting the duck with the juices every so often. Add the chestnuts for the last 20 minutes. Remove and serve hot with the gorgeous pan juices alongside.

RISOTTO AU SAFRAN ET FOIE DE CANARD POUR LE DÎNER D'ANNIVERSAIRE DE TEALDO

SAFFRON RISOTTO WITH DUCK LIVER FOR TEALDO'S BIRTHDAY DINNER

SERVES 6

good pinch of saffron
4–5 tbsp olive oil
4 banana shallots or 9–10 regular shallots, diced
2 cloves garlic, diced
2¼ cups (16 oz/500 g) Arborio rice
1⅔ cups (13 fl oz/400 ml) dry white wine
8 cups (64 fl oz/2 l) good-quality chicken stock
2 tsp unsalted butter
6 duck or chicken livers
grated Parmesan, to taste
1 tbsp crème fraîche
sea salt and black pepper

Donatella, my sister's godmother, taught me how to make this risotto only after I'd twisted her arm for many summers . . . but I definitely don't have the Italian flair for making it that she does. She barely even looks at what she's doing while she chats, and still manages to pull off a spectacular supper for my godfather Tealdo's birthday. The secret of a perfect risotto is stirring continuously. If you have any leftovers, you could use them to make Risotto Balls with Leek, Thyme and Fennel Seeds (page 147).

First, pour 4 tablespoons boiling water into a teacup with the saffron and leave to infuse for 10 minutes. Heat a generous drizzle of olive oil in a large saucepan over medium-high heat, add the shallots and cook until turning translucent. Add the garlic, then the rice. Pour in the wine and stir with a wooden spoon, letting the rice steam and soak up all the flavors. Keep stirring and add a quarter of the stock. Now add the infused saffron water, and as you stir, the gentle golden color will slowly seep through. Keep adding stock a little at a time to loosen the rice, stirring continuously, and after 15–20 minutes, the rice should start to become tender.

Heat another pan big enough to fit all the livers over medium heat with the butter and a splash of olive oil. Add the livers. They are extremely delicate and burn easily, so fry them quickly for 30 seconds only on each side. Remove and set aside.

Back to the golden risotto: taste to check that the rice is creamy and soft. Add a little more stock and some Parmesan. Season with salt and pepper and stir in the crème fraîche. If it needs a little loosening up, add a few tablespoons hot water. Serve with a duck liver on top.

ÉPAULE DE PORC BRAISÉE ET PÊCHE | SLOW-COOKED PORK SHOULDER WITH PEACH

SERVES 6

4 lb (2 kg) boneless pork shoulder,
in one piece
2 tbsp peanut oil
2 tbsp olive oil
5½ tbsp (2¾ oz/80 g)
unsalted butter
6 cloves garlic, sliced
zest of 1 unwaxed lemon,
pared into strips
large handful fresh sage leaves
1 cup (8 fl oz/250 ml) white wine
3 tbsp peach jam
1¼ cups (10 fl oz/300 ml)
whole milk
sea salt and black pepper

Ever since learning how to make the succulent suckling pig served at Bocca di Lupo restaurant in London, I've been obsessed with creating my own version. It's incredible with simply roasted sweet potatoes and cooked baby spinach. The peach jam brings about a sweet, sticky sauce that works an absolute dream with the meat. Make sure you look for a thick layer of fat on your pork, a sign that the meat is of good quality. Ask the butcher to remove the bone but leave on the skin.

Season the pork generously with a little peanut oil, salt and pepper. Heat a little peanut oil in a large pan, add the pork and brown on all sides. Remove and set aside. Heat the olive oil and butter over medium heat and add the garlic. Cook for a few moments, then add the lemon zest and sage and return the pork to the pan. Add a little of the white wine and reduce the heat to a gentle simmer. Cover and simmer very gently for 3 hours, turning and basting the pork well every 30 minutes and drizzling in a little more wine as you do so. During the last hour, stir in the peach jam and gradually pour in the milk. The pork is ready when it can be torn apart easily with a fork. It's important to keep the pan covered throughout the simmering process, except for a very small gap. Season again and serve with the sauces from the bottom of the pan. This. Will. Melt. In. Your. Mouth.

STEAK À LA NINA | NINA'S STEAK

SERVES 6

2 rump or sirloin steaks, about
6½ oz (200 g) each
2 tbsp peanut oil
½ tsp sea salt
black pepper

FOR THE SAUCE

1 anchovy fillet, chopped
4 tbsp (2 fl oz/60 ml) olive oil
bunch fresh tarragon leaves (about
1 cup/1¾ oz/50 g), finely chopped
handful fresh flat-leaf parsley,
finely chopped
juice of ½ lemon
½ tsp sugar
1 tbsp Muscat vinegar or
white wine vinegar
4 tsp unsalted butter
1 large clove garlic, diced
sea salt and black pepper

I once worked as a waitress at a restaurant called Le Relais de Venise, or L'Entrecôte, and I was immediately drawn to its menu, The Formula: a simple walnut salad with mustard dressing followed by steak and fries smothered in a sauce with 26 different ingredients. The sauce has stuck with me since I was 18, and after trying—unsuccessfully—to pry the secret ingredients out of one of the chefs, I have devised my own, less complicated recipe. Fries are probably this dish's best friend, but to keep it light you could serve it with grilled or roasted vegetables.

Remove the steaks from the fridge to allow them to come to room temperature. To make the sauce, put the anchovy in a bowl with all the olive oil except 1 tablespoon. Add the herbs, lemon juice, sugar and vinegar. Heat the remaining olive oil and butter in a large saucepan until hot. Add the garlic and cook for a moment before adding it to the bowl, stirring everything together and seasoning with salt and pepper. Cover and set aside to keep warm.

Wipe out the frying pan, place it over high heat and add half of the peanut oil. Season the steaks generously with salt, pepper and peanut oil. Make a few slices into the fat of each steak; this will help render the fat while frying. Once the pan is hot, use tongs to put the meat in the pan and cook for 2 minutes for rare, before turning over and cooking for 1 minute. Quickly brown the sides, then remove and set aside to rest in a warm place for at least 10 minutes.

Pour all the meat juices that have seeped out from the meat into the sauce bowl and use a sharp knife to slice the steaks. Heat the sauce in the frying pan. Mix the meat slices in with the sauce and serve sprinkled with a pinch of salt.

STEAK TARTARE ET OEUFS DE CAILLE | STEAK TARTARE WITH QUAIL EGGS

SERVES 2

6 quail eggs
2 beef fillets, 5 oz (150 g) each
1 tsp English mustard
2½ small shallots, diced
1 tsp capers, chopped
1½ tsp ketchup
2 tsp chopped fresh
flat-leaf parsley
Tabasco, to serve
sea salt and black pepper

This take on the classic dish not only looks awesome but using a different kind of egg also gives it a slightly different twist. Everyone has his or her own preference when it comes to Tabasco, so I always serve it on the side. It's extremely important to wash the quail eggshells carefully before they touch the raw meat, and to use clean knives and cutting boards at all times. The tartare is excellent with fries and equally delicious with warm toasted sourdough.

Carefully wash the quail eggs and leave them to dry on paper towels. Slice the beef fillets thinly, then cut them into lengthwise slices and then into dice. Continue chopping until the fillets combine together into a fine mince, add to a bowl with the remaining ingredients, except the eggs and Tabasco, and season with salt and pepper. Mix it all together and taste to check the seasoning. Divide the meat into round patties on two serving plates. Separate the quail eggs, keeping the yolks in their eggshell halves. Place three egg yolks in their shells on top of each tartare. Serve with Tabasco on the side. Before eating, let each guest tip and mix the yolks into their tartare. Eat immediately!

DAUBE DE TAUREAU, COMPOTE DE MÛRES ET GENIÈVRE | BULLFIGHT BEEF STEW WITH BLACKBERRY AND JUNIPER COMPOTE

SERVES 4

2 lb (1 kg) beef cheeks, cut into large chunks
2 tbsp peanut oil
6½ oz (200 g) lardons
3 red onions, diced
1 rib celery, finely chopped
8 cloves garlic, diced
3½ oz (100 g) baby carrots
¾ cup plus 1½ tbsp (6½ fl oz/200 ml) red wine
finely grated zest of 1 orange
3 bay leaves
2 tbsp fresh thyme leaves
3 qt (3 l) beef stock
1 tsp juniper berries
1 cinnamon stick
4 whole cloves
sea salt and black pepper

FOR THE BERRY COMPOTE
1 tsp juniper berries, lightly crushed
2 cups (9½ oz/300 g) blackberries
1 tbsp unrefined superfine sugar
1 tbsp freshly squeezed orange juice

This iconic dish is usually made with the cheapest cuts of meat (in some parts of France, sometimes with bulls killed during bullfighting festivals). I like to use beef cheeks, which melt in your mouth like nothing else after a long, slow cook. Juniper berries are commonly used, but I've replaced the traditional prunes with a heavenly blackberry compote. Depending on the time of year, it's served with buttery tagliatelle or silky, garlic-fried spinach.

Toss the beef cheeks in a little peanut oil and season well with salt and pepper. Heat a large saucepan over high heat, add the cheeks and fry until browned and seared, turning them with tongs, then remove and set aside. Add the lardons to the same pan and fry until lightly golden, then add the onions and cook until translucent. Add the celery, garlic and carrots and cook for a few minutes more, stirring well. Return the cheeks to the pan and add the red wine and the rest of the ingredients. Bring to a boil, reduce the heat and simmer for 3 hours, stirring every now and then for 20 minutes.

After the slow cooking, the cheeks will have transformed into wonderfully velvety segments. Strain the stew through a sieve and return the juices to high heat to reduce and thicken for about 15 minutes. Once thickened, return the meat and vegetables to the pan, discarding the bay leaves, cloves and cinnamon stick, and season with salt and pepper.

During the last 30 minutes of cooking, place a small saucepan over medium heat and add all the berry compote ingredients. Bring to a boil, then reduce the heat to a simmer, breaking up some of the berries with a fork. Taste to check the stew's seasoning one last time and serve with the berry compote.

DESERT
DESSERT

MY PASSION FOR cooking started with desserts, and the love affair began at an old ice-cream parlor in Port Grimaud called Del-Rey. I used to drive my dinghy through the canals toward this waterside paradise with a purseful of pocket money, and tuck into *pêche melba*, *café liégeois* and sundaes galore. The sweet Belgian couple who used to own the parlor concentrated on giving their customers a high-quality, classic ice cream experience. I've tried to bring it back to life here, and I insist that you try some of my all-time favorite Del-Rey dishes: Gaufre Dame-Blanche, Mont Blanc and the heavenly Banana Split.

In St. Tropez, dessert is taken very seriously. Ice-cream cone vendors bustle through town and the smell of hot vanilla waffles wafts around street corners. Strolling along with dessert while seeing the town at night is an experience that can't be missed. If I had to choose one place to go, it would be the Crêperie Grand Marnier. Located in the old town, it's run by some incredible pancake makers who cook in the sweltering summer heat over stoves sizzling with butter, Nutella and the famous orange liqueur. Here I show how a splash of this gorgeous, caramel-colored nectar enhances sauces, ganaches and fruit compotes. My neighbor's Panama Tierra dark chocolate illustrates how good-quality chocolate can effortlessly lift a recipe from ordinariness to the ultimate indulgence. And as with most recipes in this book, it's the place, person and time that inspires me to create it, from La Môle's decadent Marbled Chocolate Mousse to Marlene Féline's birthday Tarte au Citron to my Date-Night White Lady Waffle with ice cream.

TARTE TATIN DU PONTON AUX POMMES, ABRICOTS ET THYM CITRON

PONTOON TARTE TATIN WITH APPLES, APRICOTS AND LEMON THYME

SERVES 8

½ lb (250 g) fresh or frozen puff
pastry, thawed if frozen
5 firm apples, peeled, cored and
cut into wedges
4 apricots, halved and pitted
juice of ½ lemon
1 cup (6½ oz/200 g) unrefined
superfine sugar
scant 3 tbsp (1¼ oz/40 g)
unsalted butter
few sprigs fresh lemon thyme
¼ cup (1 oz/30 g) sliced almonds
3 tbsp Grand Marnier (optional)
sea salt

Anything with caramel in it and I'm there. Supposedly, the first tarte Tatin was made by mistake by the Tatin sisters back in Paris in the 1880s. What a wonderful mistake. The last time I made this, I sat eating it at the end of our pontoon, overlooking the Giscle, trying desperately to catch the last few rays of the day. This is amazing on its own or paired with Chestnut and Honey Ice Cream (page 241).

Preheat the oven to 350°F (180°C) and cut a circle of puff pastry to fit the shape of an 8-inch (20-cm) ovenproof frying pan. Cover and set aside in the fridge. Put the apples and apricots in a bowl and stir in the lemon juice. Melt the sugar, butter and a pinch of salt in the ovenproof frying pan over medium heat and cook to a golden caramel color. Add the apple segments to the pan, arranging them in a circle and fitting the apricots in the middle. The fruit should be packed tightly, so continue squeezing the fruit in until the pan is full. Sprinkle the lemon thyme leaves over the fruit, reserving a few for later, and bake for about 30 minutes.

Remove and carefully place the pastry over the top, tucking in the edges. Return the pan to the oven for another 20 minutes, until the pastry has puffed up and cooked. Remove the pan and place a serving plate face down over the pastry. Wearing oven gloves, quickly flip the tart over so that it comes out onto the plate. The fruit should be beautifully caramelized. Sprinkle with the almonds and some more thyme leaves, followed by a naughty glug of Grand Marnier, if using. Ahh, I want one!

TARTE AU CITRON ET FRUIT DE LA PASSION DE MARLÈNE | MARLÈNE'S LEMON AND PASSION FRUIT TART

SERVES 10

½ batch sweet pastry (page 110)
1 vanilla bean
3 free-range large eggs, plus 5 yolks
¾ cup plus 1 tbsp (6 oz/180 g) unrefined superfine sugar
finely grated zest of 5 unwaxed lemons, plus the juice of 2½ unwaxed lemons
1½ passion fruits, pulp scooped out
⅔ cup (5 oz/150 g) soft unsalted butter, plus extra for greasing

The classic tarte au citron *always reminds me of Marlène Féline, who lives a few doors down from me. On Marlène's birthday, her daughter Agnès goes to Grimaud to pick up her mother's favorite tart from a specific pâtisserie. My lemon tart is based on it, but I balance the lemon with passion fruit to cut through some of the acidity.*

Preheat the oven to 325°F (170°C) and grease a 10-inch (25-cm) tart pan with a removable bottom. Grate the pastry over the tart pan in an even layer and press the dough into the pan with your hands. Grate a little more for the edges and create an even layer. You may not need all the pastry. Gently prick the pastry all over with a fork and bake for about 25 minutes, until light in color but not golden. Remove and leave to cool on a wire rack. Increase the oven temperature to 450°F (230°C).

Half fill a large saucepan with water and bring to a simmer. Split the vanilla bean in half lengthwise and scrape out the seeds with the back of a knife. Place a heatproof bowl over the pan, making sure the bowl does not touch the water. Whisk the eggs, yolks and sugar in it with a handheld mixer until the sugar has dissolved. Add the lemon zest, juice, passion fruit pulp and vanilla seeds, whisking constantly to keep the eggs from curdling. The mixture will begin to thicken after about 10 minutes, and at this point whisk in half the butter. Increase the heat a little if needed. Once combined, add the rest of the butter. The whole process should take about 25 minutes. Transfer the mixture to a pitcher. Now place the pastry shell in the oven, then pour the filling into it (this will prevent any spillage). Bake for about 10–13 minutes, checking frequently. Remove when the tart is beautifully speckled with brown spots and leave to cool. Once set, remove the tart from the pan and serve or store in the fridge until needed.

PETIT GÂTEAU DU BALCON AVEC ANANAS CARAMÉLISÉ ET MASCARPONE | BALCONY CUPCAKES WITH CARAMELIZED PINEAPPLE AND MASCARPONE

MAKES 12 CUPCAKES

FOR THE CUPCAKES
¾ cup (6¼ oz/190 g) soft
unsalted butter
¾ cup plus 2 tbsp (6¼ oz/190 g)
unrefined superfine sugar
1 vanilla bean
3 free-range large eggs
3 tbsp whole milk
1 cup plus 3 tbsp (6 oz/190 g)
all-purpose flour
2 tsp baking powder
pinch of salt
1 batch Mascarpone Cream
(page 110), leaving out the
orange blossom water

FOR THE PINEAPPLE
1 small pineapple
⅓ cup (2¼ oz/70 g) unrefined
superfine sugar
4 tsp unsalted butter

After a dinner party we often gather enough energy to wind up the spiral lighthouse staircase to our balcony with a pot of tea and a plate of these bad-boy cupcakes. After which, the thought of climbing back down the corridor is a bit too much for some. I have been known to find the odd guest passed out there in the morning, cupcake in hand!

Preheat the oven to 350°F (180°C). In a stand mixer, cream the butter and sugar until light and fluffy. Split the vanilla bean in half lengthwise, scrape out the seeds with the back of a knife, and add the seeds to the mixer. In a small bowl, whisk together the eggs and milk. Now gradually add the egg and milk mixture until incorporated. In a large bowl, sift the flour, baking powder and salt. Using a metal spoon, gradually fold the flour mixture into the batter until just incorporated. Do not overmix. Line a 12-cup muffin pan with paper liners and spoon in the batter, filling about two-thirds full. Bake for about 30 minutes, until light and springy to the touch. Remove and cool on a wire rack.

Cut the top and bottom off the pineapple, slice the skin off, remove the little brown "eyes" with a small, sharp knife and chop it into large cubes, removing the core if necessary. Gently heat the sugar and butter in a frying pan and cook to a light, golden caramel; this should take about 10 minutes. Add the pineapple pieces and leave to caramelize for a few minutes; try not to move them around too much. Use tongs to turn them over and caramelize on both sides. Spoon the sauce over the fruit and increase the heat a little if needed to help it cook. Remove and set aside to cool. Slice the pieces into thin slivers. Ice the cupcakes with Mascarpone Cream, arrange the caramelized pineapple on the cream and top with any leftover caramel juices from the pan.

BROWNIES AU CHOCOLAT ET PRALINÉ DE DELPHINE | DELPHINE'S CHOCOLATE PRALINE BROWNIES

MAKES 12

4 free-range large eggs
1²/₃ cups (11½ oz/350 g) unrefined superfine sugar
½ cup (4 oz/125 g) unsalted butter
5½ oz (170 g) praline (see Hazelnut and Almond Spread, page 26)
6½ oz (200 g) dark chocolate (at least 70% cacao solids)
⅓ cup (2 oz/65 g) all-purpose flour
¾ cup plus 3 tbsp (2¾ oz/80 g) unsweetened cocoa powder
1 tsp baking powder

Delphine works at a chocolate shop called La Pause Douceur. She's a bit like Juliette Binoche in the film Chocolat, *although when I said this she asked, rightly, "So where's Johnny Depp?" She runs three shops in St. Tropez with her mother. Both of them are passionate about the quality of their chocolates, and their chocolaterie windows are beautifully designed and enticing. Chocolate and praline are the very best of friends, and they work magically together in these brownies.*

Preheat the oven to 325°F (170°C) and line a 15 x 10-inch (37 x 25-cm) baking pan with parchment paper. Whisk the eggs and sugar together until velvety and smooth; this will take about 7 minutes using a stand mixer or handheld electric mixer on a fast setting. When you lift up the whisk, the mixture should leave a thick trail.

Meanwhile, melt the butter, praline and chocolate in a heatproof bowl set over a pan of barely simmering water. Combine the flour, cocoa and baking powder in a separate large bowl. Slowly pour the melted chocolate mixture into the dry ingredients and stir until fully incorporated. Next, fold in the eggs and sugar with a spatula, making sure that everything is well mixed. Pour the batter into the prepared pan and bake for 15-20 minutes, until a delicate skin has formed on top. Remove and allow to cool completely on a wire rack before turning out and slicing into 12 brownies. They should be rich and gooey in the middle.

CHEESECAKE AU GRAND MARNIER | GRAND MARNIER CHEESECAKE

SERVES 8

FOR THE BASE
½ lb (250 g) digestive biscuits, such as McVitie's, or graham crackers
4 tbsp (2 oz/60 g) soft unsalted butter, plus extra for greasing
pinch of ground cinnamon

FOR THE CHEESECAKE
1 vanilla bean
1 lb (500 g) cream cheese (at room temperature)
½ cup plus 2 tbsp (4 oz/125 g) unrefined superfine sugar
2 free-range large eggs, plus 4 yolks
¾ cup (6 fl oz/175 ml) sour cream
finely grated zest of 1 unwaxed lemon
5 tbsp Grand Marnier
1 tsp vanilla extract
6½ tbsp (1¾ oz/50 g) pistachios, crushed

Ever since I was little, Le Crêperie Grand Marnier has been an important landmark for me. Time has not touched this place, where the chefs wear the tallest hats I've ever seen and a sweet-smelling pancake scent lures customers inside. The secret of this cheesecake is in the generous glug of the famous sweet orange liqueur. One of the many dishes you can use it in is the iconic crêpes Suzette, but for something extra-special you must try this creamy, delicate cheesecake . . . ooh là là!

Preheat the oven to 350°F (180°C) and grease a 9-inch (23-cm) springform cake pan with butter. In a food processor, pulse together the biscuits and butter until they form light crumbs. Pour the biscuit mixture into the prepared pan and flatten it over the bottom to create an even base, then sprinkle over the cinnamon. Firmly wrap the bottom half of the cake in 3 layers of aluminum foil. Set aside in the fridge to cool.

Boil some water in a tea kettle. Split the vanilla bean in half lengthwise and scrape out the seeds with the back of a knife. In a large bowl, beat the cream cheese and sugar with a handheld electric mixer until well mixed. Whisk the eggs and yolks lightly with a fork. While continuing to beat the cream cheese, slowly add the eggs and then the sour cream, lemon zest, Grand Marnier and vanilla seeds and extract. Smooth the mixture over the chilled base with a spatula and place in a deep roasting pan (at least 1½ inches/4 cm deep). Carefully pour the boiling water into the roasting pan so that it comes 1 inch (2.5 cm) up the sides of the cake pan. Bake for 30–40 minutes, or until the cheesecake forms a firm top but still has a little wobble. Toward the end of cooking, cover the cake pan with foil to prevent burning. Leave to cool, then place in the fridge for 30 minutes to set. While the cake is chilling, blitz the pistachios in a blender. Remove the cheesecake from the pan and top with a generous layer of crushed pistachios.

TOUR DE PAVLOVA DE L'ARTISTE ET CRÈME AU MARSALA

ARTIST'S PAVLOVA TOWER WITH MARSALA CREAM

SERVES 8–10

FOR THE MERINGUES
1¼ cups (10 oz/280 g) unrefined superfine sugar
½ cup plus 1 tbsp (4½ oz/140 g) egg whites (about 4 free-range large eggs)
1 tsp vanilla extract
few drops lemon juice
1 tbsp cornstarch
pinch of sea salt

FOR THE MARSALA CREAM
scant 2 cups (14½ fl oz/450 ml) heavy cream
⅓ cup (2¼ oz/70 g) unrefined confectioners' sugar
3 tbsp (1½ fl oz/45 ml) sweet Marsala wine

FOR THE FRUIT
rounded 1 cup (5 oz/150 g) blueberries
¾ cup (3½ oz/100 g) cherries
⅔ cup (3½ oz/100 g) blackberries
3 cups (13 oz/400 g) raspberries
3 cups (13 oz/400 g) strawberries
unrefined confectioners' sugar, for dusting

I once filled my van's cake counter with gigantic meringues for a party. One man in particular, an artist, loved them so much that he wanted to cast one in bronze for a sculpture. He was so enthusiastic about the idea that he wanted to create a meringue tower. Oswaldo Macia, this dinner party showstopper is for you. The meringues should be made the night before.

Preheat the oven to 400°F (200°C) and line two sheet pans with parchment paper. Pour the sugar for the meringue into one pan and place in the oven for 10 minutes to warm up. Meanwhile, whisk the egg whites, salt, vanilla extract and lemon juice in a stand mixer until they form stiff peaks. Continue to mix and add the hot sugar, a spoonful at a time, making sure to incorporate each spoonful fully before adding the next. Only stop mixing when the meringues are firm and you can hold the bowl over your head without anything falling out. This will take about 10 minutes. Reduce the oven temperature to 250°F (130°C). Lightly fold the cornstarch into the whites with a large spoon. Tip half the meringue mixture onto a prepared sheet pan, spreading it out to create a bowl shape. Now use the remaining mixture to create two smaller meringue-shaped bowls, one smaller than the other, on the second pan. You should be left with three meringue bowls on the pans, all different sizes. Bake for 3 hours. Turn off the oven and leave the meringues inside it to dry out overnight.

Whip together all the ingredients for the cream and store in the fridge until needed. Assemble the tower just before serving by building each layer from largest to smallest, layering generously with the cream followed by an assortment of fruit. Lightly dust with confectioners' sugar and serve immediately.

BOCCONOTTO | ALMOND AND RHUBARB TARTLETS

MAKES 12

FOR THE RHUBARB
6 oz (180 g) rhubarb
(about 2 sticks), sliced into
1¼-inch (3-cm) chunks
4½ tbsp (2 oz/60 g) unrefined
superfine sugar
2 tbsp lemon juice

FOR THE BOCCONOTTO
½ cup plus 1 tsp (4¼ oz/130 g) soft
unsalted butter, plus
extra for greasing
6½ tbsp (3 oz/85 g) unrefined
superfine sugar
1 free-range large egg plus
1 yolk, lightly beaten
3 tbsp (1 oz/30 g) all-purpose flour
¼ cup (2 oz/60 g) ground almonds
1 tbsp Grand Marnier or Amaretto
confectioners' sugar, for dusting
vanilla ice cream, to serve
(optional)

This is another classic I learned at L'Anima restaurant in London. Bocconotto is a type of pastry typically found in the Italian regions of Puglia, Abruzzo and Calabria, where my boss Francesco Mazzei is from. It is traditionally filled with chocolate, cinnamon or almonds, and Mazzei used the latter. 'Forza Calabria!'

Put the rhubarb in a saucepan with the sugar and lemon juice, place over low heat and simmer gently for 10-15 minutes. Remove and set aside to cool.

Preheat the oven to 325°F (170°C) and lightly butter 12 small, nonstick brioche molds. Cream the butter and sugar in a stand mixer until light and airy. Continue at medium speed and slowly add the egg and yolk, making sure all is combined. Reduce the speed and sift in the flour and then stir in the ground almonds and liqueur. Put a heaped teaspoon of the batter into each mold, giving it a tap against the surface to get rid of any air bubbles. Add a level teaspoon of the rhubarb mixture on top of the batter, then add a little more batter to cover the rhubarb (fill no more than two-thirds full). Give all the molds another tap. Bake for 40-45 minutes, or until the tops are golden. Remove and cool on a wire rack for about 15 minutes, then gently pry the tartlets out of the molds and leave to cool completely. Dust generously with confectioners' sugar and serve with vanilla ice cream if you like.

LE FAMEUX GÂTEAU AU CHOCOLAT ET AUX NOIX DE BUBI | BUBI'S FAMOUS CHOCOLATE WALNUT CAKE

SERVES 10

2 cups (14½ oz/450 g) unrefined superfine sugar
9 free-range large eggs, separated
2¾ cups (11 oz/340 g) walnuts, finely chopped, plus rounded ½ cup (2 oz/60 g) walnut halves, to decorate
3 tbsp dried bread crumbs
2 batches Panna Tierra Chocolate Sauce (page 232), cooled completely

My grandmother Bubi was Polish, and every birthday she would whip up this rich, nutty, super-silky Polish creation. I can remember one time when she chopped the walnuts for hours in the garden, with such care and precision. I fell asleep listening to the clinking of her gold bracelets, only to be woken up by yet more chopping. Sadly, Bubi didn't write down the recipe very clearly for me, and it's taken quite a few trials to get it just right. I hope this version would make her proud.

Preheat the oven to 325°F (170°C) and line two 8-inch (20-cm) springform cake pans with parchment paper. Using a stand mixer or handheld electric mixer, beat half the sugar with the egg yolks until pale. Stir in the chopped walnuts and bread crumbs and transfer to a mixing bowl. In a clean and dry mixing bowl, whisk the egg whites to form stiff peaks. It will take about 12 minutes to whip enough air into them to make them firm. Slowly spoon in the remaining sugar until all is mixed in. Now fold a third of the egg whites into the walnut batter and then combine another third and then finally the last. Carefully divide between the two cake pans and bake for 50 minutes to 1 hour, or until the top is firm and a skewer inserted into the cake comes out almost clean. Do not open the oven until nearly the end of the cooking time. Remove and leave to cool on a wire rack before carefully taking out of the pans. Leave to cool to room temperature. The cake has a meringue-like structure, so it may appear cracked at the top.

Spread the chocolate sauce over the surface of the cooked cakes and place one on top of the other. Ice the edges and decorate with the walnut halves. Serve immediately. It will keep, covered and at room temperature, for up to 4 days.

GÂTEAU AU CHOCOLAT À LA MAGIE NOIRE | BLACK MAGIC CHOCOLATE CAKE

SERVES 20

1 batch The Birthday Cake sponge, with half the amount of icing (page 118)
1 vanilla bean
1¼ cups (10 fl oz/300 ml) double cream
2 tbsp unrefined confectioners' sugar
2 cups (8 oz/250 g) raspberries

FOR THE BLUEBERRY COMPOTE
rounded 1 cup (5 oz/150 g) blueberries
2 tsp unrefined superfine sugar
few drops lemon juice

FOR THE VANILLA-SOAKED FIGS
2 vanilla beans
8 small Black Mission figs, quartered
1 tbsp light brown muscovado sugar
1–2 tbsp Amaretto

I love it when a person inspires a dish. My old friend Drum is a spectacular and extremely talented magician and, wherever Drum goes, magic is not far behind. Extravagant, mysterious, heavenly to look at . . . and the cake isn't bad either!

Bake the cake in two 9½-inch (24-cm) cake pans and make the icing.

Put the blueberries, sugar and lemon juice in a small saucepan and set over medium heat. Stir them around for 10–12 minutes, until you have a jam consistency. Set aside to cool.

Now for the figs: split the vanilla beans in half lengthwise and scrape out the seeds with the back of a knife. Put the figs, vanilla seeds and pods, muscovado sugar and Amaretto in a large frying pan and place over medium-low heat. Gently dissolve the sugar and simmer for no longer than 7 minutes. Set aside and allow the fruit to cool completely.

To make the vanilla cream, split the vanilla bean in half lengthwise and scrape out the seeds with the back of a knife. Whisk the cream, confectioners' sugar and vanilla seeds together until light and fluffy.

To assemble the cake, place one of the chocolate sponges on a serving plate, using two large knives tucked under each other at angles to make it easier to move. Be sure to have the neatest and flattest side of this sponge facing up. Divide the chocolate icing between the two halves, spreading it with the back of a spoon to create lovely waves. Divide the vanilla cream between the two sponges, layering it on top of the chocolate. Drizzle the blueberry compote over the sponge on the serving plate and arrange the raspberries on top. Carefully sit the other sponge on top of the raspberries. Arrange the fig quarters in the center, spoon on any sauce from the pan and scatter the vanilla pods on top to garnish.

MOUSSE AU CHOCOLAT MARBRÉE DE LA MÔLE | LA MÔLE'S MARBLED CHOCOLATE MOUSSE

SERVES 8-10

1 cup (8 fl oz/250 ml) whole milk
3 free-range large eggs, separated
¼ cup (1¾ oz/50 g) unrefined
superfine sugar
½ cup (2 oz/60 g) cornstarch
1 tbsp unsweetened cocoa powder
few drops lemon juice
pinch of salt
1 cup (4¼ oz/130 g) unrefined
confectioners' sugar
5 oz (150 g) dark chocolate,
plus 1¾ oz (50 g) for grating
(at least 70% cacao solids)
¾ cup plus 2 tbsp (7 fl oz/200 ml)
heavy cream
1 tbsp Amaretto or Grand Marnier

For me, only one chocolate mousse cuts the mustard, a homemade one inspired by our local restaurant, La Môle. This marbled mousse is a striking dessert to bring to the dinner table in a large glass bowl.

Begin by making a pastry cream: warm the milk in a large saucepan over medium heat. Whisk together the egg yolks and sugar in a bowl until pale, then stir in the cornstarch and cocoa powder. Slowly pour in the warm milk a little at a time until it is all incorporated. Return the mixture to the pan and place over medium-high heat, whisking constantly to prevent the eggs from curdling. Stir until it thickens and bubbles, then use a spatula to scrape it into a clean bowl. Cover with plastic wrap touching the surface of the cream to prevent a skin from forming. Set aside to cool.

Pour the egg whites, lemon juice and salt into a stand mixer and beat to stiff peaks. Continue at a fast speed, slowly adding the confectioners' sugar until glossy. Meanwhile, break the chocolate into a heatproof bowl and set it over a pan of barely simmering water to melt, then remove from the heat. In a separate bowl, whisk the heavy cream until light and fluffy. At this point you should have four bowls of different ingredients. Loosen the pastry cream by stirring with a spatula, and add the liqueur. Stir the melted chocolate into the pastry cream. Clean the spatula and carefully fold the whipped cream into the egg whites. Fold half the white mixture into the chocolate mixture, until completely mixed, taking care not to lose too much air. Put a couple of spoonfuls of the chocolate mousse in a serving bowl, followed by a few of the white mixture. Use the spatula to mix and marble everything together. Continue adding and mixing, leaving some unmixed darker and whiter parts all over. Finish with a generous grating of dark chocolate on top. Allow the mousse to set in the fridge for 1 hour before serving. It will keep in the fridge for no more than 2 days.

SAUCE AU CHOCOLAT PANNA TIERRA | PANNA TIERRA CHOCOLATE SAUCE

**MAKES 1⅔ CUPS
(13 FL OZ/400 ML)**

¾ cup plus 2 tbsp (6½ fl oz/
200 ml) heavy cream
6 tbsp plus 1 tsp (2¾ oz/80 g)
unrefined superfine sugar
3¾ oz (110 g) dark chocolate
(at least 70% cacao solids),
roughly chopped
2 tsp unsalted butter

Since the early days at Port Grimaud's special ice cream parlor Del-Rey, when it would arrive in a little white jug to accompany a waffle, crêpe or sundae, warm chocolate sauce has been a top priority. This recipe makes the ultimate chocolate sauce, and once cooled it can be used to ice cakes and tarts. The formula here is simple. Find a heavenly, bursting-with-flavor dark chocolate, then feast to your heart's content on this sauce. Spooning from the jug is completely justifiable, and sometimes necessary.

Heat the cream and sugar in a saucepan until the sugar has dissolved. Add the chocolate and stir until melted and combined, then remove from the heat and stir in the butter. C'est tout!

GLACE À LA VANILLE DE MADAGASCAR | MADAGASCAN VANILLA ICE CREAM

**MAKES 6 CUPS
(48 FL OZ/1.5 L)**

3 cups (24 fl oz/750 ml) whole milk
1 cup (8 fl oz/250 ml) heavy cream
2 vanilla beans
½ cup plus 1½ tbsp (5 oz/150 g)
egg yolks (8-9 free-range
large eggs)
¾ cup (5 oz/150 g) unrefined
superfine sugar

Vanilla is the best flavor when it comes to homemade ice cream. Speckled all over with jet-black vanilla seeds, it is very beautiful. My love affair with vanilla ice cream began at Del-Rey, a three-minute boat ride from my house in Port Grimaud, where my sister and I would spend our pocket money. If you have an ice cream machine it will give you a slightly better texture. Serve it with my signature Panna Tierra Chocolate Sauce (opposite).

Heat the milk and cream in a large saucepan over medium heat. Split the vanilla beans in half lengthwise and scrape out the seeds with the back of a knife. Add the seeds and vanilla pods to the pan and simmer very gently for about 15 minutes. Meanwhile, prepare a bowl with a sieve set over it. In another large bowl, whisk the yolks and sugar together until pale. Slowly add a little of the hot milk, whisking constantly, then return the mixture to the pan. Return to medium heat and cook, still whisking, until it reaches 180°F (82°C) using a thermometer or until thick enough to coat the back of a wooden spoon.

Pour the mixture through the sieve. Use a spoon to push through any lumps and discard the vanilla pods, then cover with plastic wrap touching the surface of the liquid to prevent a skin from forming. Leave to cool to room temperature before churning in an ice cream machine. Scoop out into a plastic container and freeze for at least 2 hours. Alternatively, once the mixture has cooled, pour it straight into a plastic container and freeze for 20 minutes. Mix with a fork and return to the freezer for 15 minutes. Continue doing this at 15-20 minute intervals until it firms up, then serve when needed. It keeps in the freezer for up to 2 months.

BANANA SPLIT À LA DEL-REY AVEC SAUCE DULCE DE LECHE ET NOIX DE MACADAMIA CARAMELISÉES

BANANA SPLIT DEL-REY STYLE WITH DULCE DE LECHE SAUCE AND CARAMELIZED MACADAMIA NUTS

SERVES 4

6½ tbsp (3½ fl oz/100 ml) condensed milk
½ cup (3½ oz/100 g) unrefined superfine sugar
2 tbsp plus 2 tsp (1¼ fl oz/40 ml) water
3 cups (2 oz/60 g) macadamia nuts
(6½ fl oz/200 ml) Chantilly Cream (page 241)
Madagascan Vanilla Ice Cream (page 233) or good-quality store-bought ice cream
4 bananas

I remember this being my flavor of the month for a few weeks, before I moved on to waffles. The dulce de leche sauce and caramelized macadamia nuts really do take the biscuit. They are so good!

Preheat the oven to 400°F (200°C) and pour the condensed milk into a small baking pan. Place it in a larger pan and pour in boiling water to come ¾ inch (2 cm) up the sides. Cover the smaller pan with aluminum foil and bake for about 2 hours. Check after 1 hour to see if the milk is turning brown. Continue to cook until it changes to a caramel color, then remove and leave to cool. Briefly give the caramel a good mix to bring it all together.

Line a sheet pan with parchment paper. Heat the sugar and water in a saucepan over medium-high heat. When the sugar begins to turn a golden caramel, remove from the heat and quickly stir in the nuts with a wooden spoon, making sure to coat all the nuts. Scrape the mixture out onto the parchment paper and leave to cool. Once cooled, peel off the paper and roughly chop into bite-sized pieces.

To assemble the banana splits, place two neat scoops of ice cream on a plate and spoon two mounds of Chantilly Cream next to the ice cream. Slice a banana in half lengthwise and place a piece on either side of the line of ice cream and cream. Sprinkle with the caramelized macadamia nuts and scatter over dollops of the dulce de leche sauce. Serve immediately.

GLACE AU CHOCOLAT PANNA TIERRA DE NORERO | THE NOREROS' PANNA TIERRA CHOCOLATE ICE CREAM

**MAKES 6 CUPS
(48 FL OZ/1.5 L)**

3⅓ cups (27 fl oz/825 ml)
heavy cream
1⅔ cups (13 fl oz/400 ml)
whole milk
½ cup plus 1½ tbsp (5 oz/150 g)
egg yolks (8–9 free-range
large eggs)
1¾ cups (11½ oz/360 g) unrefined
superfine sugar
¾ lb (12 oz/380 g) Duffy's Panama
Tierra Oscura chocolate, roughly
chopped (or any other good-
quality dark chocolate with 70%
cacao solids, such as Valrhona)
1 tbsp Amaretto (optional)

This has made people who say they don't even like ice cream call me up the next day to ask when they can get some more. I think it's the incredible chocolate that comes from the Noreros, an Ecuadorian family who used to be our neighbors on La Giscle. They have a cacao bean plantation in Ecuador, and luckily they supply a magician of a man in the UK named Duffy. In his small, old-fashioned factory he turns these beautiful beans into a bar of dark chocolate called Panama Tierra Oscura, which means "dark earth." When an order arrives in the mail, it's a wonderful experience in itself, as the bars are wrapped simply in white newspaper. I gave it the pet name "Panna Tierra" and am addicted to it for its quality and sheer depth of flavor.

Heat the cream and milk in a large saucepan over medium heat. In a large bowl, whisk together the yolks and sugar until pale. Slowly pour a little of the hot milk and cream mixture into the bowl and whisk well. Continue adding and stirring gradually until everything is combined. Pour the mixture back into the saucepan and cook over medium-high heat, stirring constantly, until the mixture reaches 180°F (82°C) using a thermometer. Remove from the heat and begin adding the chocolate and the Amaretto (if using), stirring until everything is incorporated. Use a spatula to scrape the mixture into a bowl and cover with plastic wrap touching the surface to prevent a skin from forming. Leave to cool to room temperature before churning in an ice cream machine. Once churned, scoop it into a plastic container and freeze for at least 2 hours. Alternatively, once the mixture has cooled, pour it straight into a plastic container and freeze for 20 minutes. Mix with a fork and return to the freezer for 15 minutes. Continue doing this at 15–20 minute intervals until it firms up. It keeps in the freezer for up to 2 months. Serve piled high with the Chestnut and Honey Ice Cream (page 241).

GLACE AU CARAMEL À LA FLEUR DE SEL | SEA-SALT CARAMEL ICE CREAM

MAKES JUST OVER 1 QT (1 L)

FOR THE MILK BASE
2 cups (16 fl oz/500 ml) whole milk
¾ cup plus 1½ tbsp (6½ fl oz/
200 ml) heavy cream
½ cup plus 1½ tbsp (5 oz/150 g)
egg yolks (8–9 free-range
large eggs)
½ tsp sea salt

FOR THE CARAMEL
1¼ cups (8 oz/250 g) unrefined
superfine sugar

Despite my enthusiasm for vanilla ice cream and chocolate sauce, when I sell sea-salt caramel flavor from my Citroën van, it sells like nothing else—like lightning!

Put the milk and cream in a pitcher and lightly beat the yolks in a large heatproof bowl. Put the sugar in a medium-sized saucepan and swirl the pan around, making sure the sugar dissolves. Cook over medium-high heat until it turns to a caramel, about 10 minutes. Keep an eye on the pan at all times, as caramel can burn within seconds. Do not stir, as this may create crystals and you need it to be smooth and silky. As soon as the caramel is a dark golden color, remove it from the heat. Wrap a tea towel around your hand and slowly pour in the cream and milk, whisking constantly. It will bubble and steam vigorously, but persist until all is combined. Slowly pour the mixture into the eggs, whisking constantly so that the eggs don't curdle. Return the mixture to the pan, place over medium-high heat and cook, whisking continuously, until it reaches 180°F (82°C) using a thermometer or until the mixture coats the back of a wooden spoon.

Strain the mixture into a bowl and add the sea salt. Taste and add more salt if needed. Cover with plastic wrap touching the surface to prevent a skin from forming. Leave to cool to room temperature before churning in an ice cream machine. Once churned, scoop into a plastic container and freeze for at least 2 hours. Alternatively, once the mixture has cooled, pour it into a plastic container and freeze for 20 minutes. Mix with a fork and return to the freezer for 15 minutes. Continue doing this at 15–20 minute intervals until it firms up. It keeps in the freezer for up to 2 months.

GLACE AU MARRON ET AU MIEL | CHESTNUT AND HONEY ICE CREAM

MAKES 1 QT (1 L)

½ cup (4 fl oz/125 ml) heavy cream
2 cups (16 fl oz/500 ml) whole milk
⅓ cup (3 fl oz/85 ml) honey
⅓ cup (2¾ oz/80 g) egg yolks
(4–5 free-range large eggs)
6½ tbsp (3 oz/90 g) unrefined
superfine sugar
½ cup (4 oz/125 g) unsweetened
chestnut purée (if sweetened,
reduce the sugar to
⅓ cup/2¼ oz/70 g)

This ice cream, combined with the Panna Tierra Chocolate Ice Cream (page 238) and Chantilly Cream (see below), is my version of the classic Mont Blanc, which my sister Juliana raves about. Serve it with toasted sliced almonds on top. It's also fantastic with my Panna Tierra Chocolate Sauce (page 232). Do it!

In a large saucepan over medium heat, heat the cream, milk and honey. In a large bowl, whisk the yolks and sugar until pale, then whisk in the chestnut purée. Trickle a little of the hot milk and cream into the egg mixture and stir until combined. Continue adding the milk mixture little by little until it is fully incorporated, then return it to the pan and increase the temperature, whisking constantly. Cook until the mixture reaches 180°F (82°C) using a thermometer or until it coats the back of a wooden spoon, then remove from the heat. Pour the thickened mixture into a bowl and leave to cool to room temperature before churning in an ice cream machine. Once the ice cream is churned, scoop it out into a plastic container and freeze for at least 2 hours. Alternatively, once the mixture has cooled, pour it straight into a plastic container and freeze for 20 minutes. Mix it with a fork and freeze for 15 minutes. Continue doing this in 15–20 minute intervals until it firms up. It keeps in the freezer for up to 2 months.

CHANTILLY CREAM

MAKES ABOUT 400 ML

1 vanilla bean
¾ cup plus 2 tbsp (6½ fl oz/
200 ml) heavy cream
1 tbsp unrefined
confectioners' sugar

Split the vanilla bean in half lengthwise and scrape out the seeds with the back of a knife. Whisk together the heavy cream, vanilla seeds and confectioners' sugar until light and delightfully fluffy. Do not overwhip.

CITRON ET THYM | LEMON AND THYME SORBET

MAKES 1½ QT (1.5 L)

Tony Parker (my dad) is obsessed! Need I say more?

3¼ cups (26 fl oz/810 ml) water
1 cup (8 fl oz/250 ml)
liquid glucose
1¼ cups (8 oz/250 g) unrefined
superfine sugar
finely grated zest of 5–6
unwaxed lemons, plus 1 cup
(8 fl oz/250 ml) juice
½ tsp fresh thyme leaves

Place the water, glucose and sugar in a large saucepan and bring to a boil. When the sugar has dissolved, remove from the heat and stir in the lemon juice, zest and thyme. Leave to cool before churning in an ice cream machine. Once churned, scrape into a plastic container and freeze for at least 1 hour. Alternatively, if you don't have an ice cream machine, pour the mixture straight into a container and freeze for 20 minutes. Mix with a fork and return to the freezer for 15 minutes. Continue doing this at 15–20 minute intervals until it firms up. It keeps in the freezer for up to 2 months.

GLACE MIEL-LAVANDE | HONEY-LAVENDER ICE CREAM

MAKES 2 QT (2 L)

This ice cream is heavenly served with La Maman's Apricot Tart (page 104).

1 cup (8 fl oz/250 ml) heavy cream
4 cups (32 fl oz/1 l) whole milk
1 cup (8 fl oz/250 ml) honey
½ cup plus 1½ tbsp (5 oz/150 g)
egg yolks (8–9 free-range
large eggs)
½ cup (3½ oz/100 g) unrefined
superfine sugar
1 tsp lavender flowers

Pour the cream, milk and honey in a saucepan and bring to a light simmer, then remove from the heat. In a heatproof bowl, whisk the egg yolks and sugar until the mixture turns pale. Carefully pour in a little of the hot cream and whisk in vigorously. Continue adding a little cream at a time until combined. Return the mixture to the saucepan along with the lavender and set over medium-high heat, whisking constantly. Cook until the mixture reaches 180°F (82°C) using a themometer or until it coats the back of a wooden spoon. Remove from the heat and leave to cool completely before churning in an ice cream machine. Once churned, scrape into a plastic container and freeze for at least 2 hours. Alternatively, if you don't have an ice cream machine, once cooled, pour the mixture straight into a container and freeze for 15 minutes. Mix with a fork and return to the freezer for 15 minutes. Continue doing this at 15–20 minute intervals until it firms up. It keeps in the freezer for up to 2 months.

PÊCHE MELBA | PEACH MELBA

This is another Del-Rey favorite, which used to hang on their ice cream wall of fame. Instead of the usual vanilla ice cream, though, my version uses only fruit. Once you have everything ready, divide a couple of scoops of peach sorbet between two bowls, top with the poached peaches and finish with a generous splash of raspberry coulis and a few lavender flowers.

WHITE PEACH SORBET

MAKES 2 QT (2 L)

about ½ cup (3½–4 oz/100–120 g)
unrefined superfine sugar
7–8 very soft white peaches
juice of ½ lemon

FOR THE SYRUP
1 cup (8 fl oz/250 ml) water
¾ cup (5¾ fl oz/175 ml)
liquid glucose
¾ cup plus 1 tbsp (5½ oz/165 g)
unrefined superfine sugar

Begin by making the sorbet syrup. Put the water, glucose and sugar in a large saucepan over high heat. Stir and just bring to a boil, then remove and leave to cool. Pit the peaches and place the flesh and skins in a bowl, then blend to a purée. Put a sieve over a large bowl, pass the purée through it and add a teaspoon or two of the leftover skins to the purée. Stir in 2 cups (16 fl oz/ 500 ml) of the sorbet syrup, the lemon juice and, depending on the sweetness of the peaches, about ½ cup (100–120 g) sugar. Stir well and taste. The sorbet should have a sweet aftertaste that will balance out once frozen. Scrape the mixture into an ice cream machine and churn. Once churned, place in a plastic container and freeze for 1 hour to set. If you don't have a machine, pour it straight into the plastic container and freeze for 20 minutes. Mix with a fork and freeze for 15 minutes. Continue doing this in 15–20 minute intervals until it firms up. It keeps in the freezer for up to 2 months.

PEACHES POACHED IN CHAMPAGNE AND LAVENDER

SERVES 2

1 large white peach, sliced into
segments
¾ cup plus 2 tsp (6½ fl oz/200 ml)
champagne or sparkling wine
½ tsp unrefined superfine sugar
½ tsp lavender flowers

Place the peach segments in a small frying pan with the champagne or sparkling wine, sugar and lavender. Place over medium-low heat and cut out a cartouche (parchment paper lid cut to fit the size of the pan with a small hole in the middle). Place the cartouche in the pan so it touches the fruit (any steam will be released through the hole). Cook gently for 10–15 minutes, until the peaches have softened and soaked up the beautiful juices. Remove and leave to cool in the pan for about 30 minutes, then serve when needed.

RASPBERRY COULIS

SERVES 2

1¼ cups (5 oz/150 g) raspberries
1–2 tsp unrefined superfine sugar
few drops lemon juice
½ tsp vanilla extract

Use a stick blender to blend the raspberries to a pulp, then pass through a sieve to remove the seeds. Add a little sugar, depending on how sweet the fruit is. Stir in the lemon juice and vanilla and store in the fridge until needed.

GAUFRE DAME-BLANCHE POUR UNE SOIRÉE EN AMOUREUX | DATE-NIGHT WHITE LADY WAFFLE

SERVES 2 (MAKES 6)

FOR THE WAFFLES
2 cups (16 fl oz/500 ml) whole milk
1 vanilla bean
2 cups (9½ oz/300 g) all-purpose flour
1 tsp baking powder
½ tsp baking soda
pinch of salt
2 free-range large eggs, separated
2 tbsp unrefined superfine sugar
7 tbsp (3½ oz/100 g) unsalted butter, melted
1–2 tbsp Amaretto, Grand Marnier or rum

FOR THE TOPPING
2 scoops Madagascan Vanilla Ice Cream (page 233), or good-quality store-bought ice cream
2 tbsp Chantilly Cream (page 241) or whipped cream
confectioners' sugar, for dusting
1½ batches Panna Tierra Chocolate Sauce (page 232)
handful toasted sliced almonds

I once went on a date with a French boy named Thomas. I was 16, he was 18 and he took me out to Del-Rey for some ice cream. As you can imagine, this was the way to my heart. The date got even better when we ordered a gaufre dame-blanche each. A heavenly, light, fluffy-yet-crunchy, sweet vanilla waffle with a scoop of ice cream, freshly whipped cream and a hot pot of silky chocolate sauce to smother all over it. You will need a waffle maker.

Preheat the waffle maker to medium-high. Warm the milk in a saucepan. Split the vanilla bean in half lengthwise, scrape out the seeds with the back of a knife and add them to the pan along with the pods. Simmer the milk gently for about 10 minutes. Meanwhile, mix the flour, baking powder, baking soda and salt in a bowl. In a separate bowl, whisk the egg whites to stiff peaks, then fold in the sugar until combined. Add the yolks to the flour bowl, then gradually add the milk mixture (having removed the vanilla pods), then stir in the melted butter, saving a teaspoon for use later, and the liqueur. Use a spatula to gently fold in the egg whites, but do not overmix.

Lightly grease the waffle maker with the reserved melted butter. Spoon in the batter and gently close the lid and cook for about 4 minutes. To assemble, position a cooked waffle on a plate and add a scoop of ice cream on one side and a generous spoonful of the cream on the other. Dust with confectioners' sugar and pour the chocolate sauce on top. Sprinkle with sliced almonds and serve extra sauce on the side for *un petit supplément*.

INDEX

ACKNOWLEDGMENTS

The idea for this book started life when I was sitting in a hammock overlooking the Giscle canal one afternoon with my sister, Juliana, and her husband, Josh. I am still pinching myself that I was lucky enough to get the chance to write it. It has been an amazing journey, with many, many, many incredible helpers along the way.

I would like to thank my mum and dad for being the most supportive parents on the planet: La Maman for believing that I can do absolutely anything I want and my dad for keeping my countless ideas in check and making sure everything is legal. No more raspberries, I promise! Thanks also to the following:

Hellie Ogden for finding me in the first place and for seeing the potential. If it wasn't for the encouragement and planting the idea to write a cookbook, I don't think I'd be here just yet. Look how far we've come! Amanda Harris for daring to take a risk on me, for sharing my vision right from the start and allowing me so much creative control. I feel we've really made something special. Kate Wanwimolruk for organizing, remaining calm and patient at all times, and for being so accommodating with my mountain of requests.

Juliana for being my creative director, sharing in all of the book excitement and being my best friend since I came onto the scene. Without you this book would absolutely not have happened or have been half as beautiful. Josh, for helping me create a strong brand; your advertising expertise has been invaluable. My brother, Christian, for driving with me to every event with the van, from the very first festival at The Secret Garden Party to following me around filming at the food shoots. You have been the chilled-out guy to have around at stressful times. My other brother, Adam, for helping me develop my recipes, encouraging me to make them as original as they could be and of course being a taste-tester.

Bubi, my grandmother, for introducing me to new tastes back when I was a fussy eater. I wish you knew how adventurous I am now. A large part of this book is for you.

Roxy First for listening for hours, providing advice and in general being a great buddy.

Francesco Mazzei from L'Anima for giving me my first job in a kitchen and memorable teachings from Lello, Antonio, Claudio, Luca and Valerio. Jacob Kennedy and the wonderful team at Bocca di Lupo/Gelato.

Team Paul: Paul Winch-Furness for making my food look mouthwatering and marvelous with just one effortless click. The photos speak for themselves, and they are better than I could have imagined. Jay and Jacob for all of your hard work on this project, and I look forward to another sours party soon! Ivar Wigan, for our exciting St. Tropez shoot. Those photos perfectly capture the stunning St. Tropez that I have known all my life. Well done for putting up with the Parkers. It was a truly special time for all of us. All of the driving, jumping, chatting up strangers, picking the perfect peach was completely worth it! Henrietta Clancy for being my rock on the food shoots; I hope that we can work together again soon. Lucien, le meilleur pêcheur du monde, merci pour tous et bien sûr, pour les instructions pour attraper un poisson! C'était un vrai miracle! Patrice De Colmont pour les entretiens, photos et plein de déjeuners de bonheur avec ma famille dans un restaurant qui a une belle histoire. The Juliette Binoche of St. Tropez, Delphine, for your out-of-this-world chocolates, and to the generous gentlemen at Crêperie Grand Marnier. Patrice for a ride in your bangin' XK 150. Captain Andreas for lending us your precious Riva on a gorgeous sunny morning.

It has been a challenging and ridiculously exciting experience and I hope this is only the first chapter.